The 1955 Brooklyn Dodgers - My Dad's Team

Len Ferman - The Sports Time Traveler

THE SPORTS TIME TRAVELER, LLC

The author certifies that he did not use artificial intelligence in researching, writing, editing or any other aspect of publishing this book.

Paperback ISBN 979-8-9915012-4-8

Ebook ISBN 979-8-9915012-5-5

Published by The Sports Time Traveler, LLC

To my dad, Stanley, a true Brooklyn Dodgers fan, and a great family man and father.

Acknowledgements

I wish to thank the following people for their contributions to this book:

Heather Ferman, my wife, who provided constant encouragement throughout this endeavor.

Arlene Ferman, my mom, who has been so supportive of all my writing.

Dr. Ron Elinoff, a Brooklyn Dodgers fan in his boyhood and the biggest Los Angeles Dodgers fan I know in the present time.

Ted Kubiak, who played on all three Oakland A's consecutive World Series championship teams from 1972 – 1974.

Peter Bavasi, son of 1955 Dodgers general manager Buzzie Bavasi. Peter is also the former president of the Toronto Blue Jays and Cleveland Indians.

Jon Weisman, Vice President, Communications of the Los Angeles Dodgers.

Marty Appel, prolific baseball author, Emmy award winning producer of New York Yankees TV broadcasts, and former Yankees public relations director.

Tom Villante, former producer and director of Brooklyn Dodgers TV and radio broadcasts from 1952 – 1958.

Claudette Scrafford, Manager of the Dean O. Cochran, Jr. Archives for the National Baseball Hall of Fame and Museum.

Steve Wejroch, photo archivist for the National Baseball Hall of Fame and Museum.

Pat Salerno, the biggest Johnny Podres fan on the planet.

FOREWORD

By Tom Villante

In 1955, the Brooklyn Dodgers got off to a terrific start.

They were a powerhouse loaded with all-stars including Jackie Robinson, Pee Wee Reese, Duke Snider, Roy Campanella, Carl Furillo, Gil Hodges, Don Newcombe and Carl Erskine.

The experts predicted they would easily win the National League pennant.

Walter O'Malley, owner of the Dodgers, was a visionary... but practical.

He visualized the Dodgers winning the 1955 National League Championship.

He visualized the Dodgers playing the New York Yankees in the 1955 World Series.

He visualized the Dodgers ...once again...losing the World Series to the Yankees.

O'Malley knew very well the disappointment of not winning the World Series and not getting that precious World Series ring.

He had an idea.

Plan B – create an alternative to a World Series ring.

A new, specially designed Brooklyn Dodgers "Organization Ring"... to be given to key Dodgers executives during the 1955 season. And, given to the Dodgers' players in October... if they lost the 1955 World Series.

Either way, the Dodgers' players would definitely get a ring in 1955... either a World Series ring... or the new Dodgers Organization ring.

A small number of Dodgers executives were given the Dodgers Organization Ring... including me.

I never caught a ball... or got a hit. Yet, in July 1955, O'Malley presented me with that special Brooklyn Dodgers Organization Ring.

I was surprised, thrilled and honored to be considered part of the Dodger family...even though I worked at BBDO Ad Agency.

I was the producer of the Dodgers TV and Radio broadcasts from 1952-1958. Schaefer Beer and Lucky Strikes cigarettes, BBDO Clients, were the sole sponsors.

Ironically, sports memorabilia experts believe the 1955 Brooklyn Dodgers Organization Ring may be rarer... and, probably more valuable than any World Series ring.

THE 1955 BROOKLYN DODGERS – MY DAD'S TEAM brought back vivid memories of being part of baseball history... living day-by-day with those great Brooklyn Dodger players.

It is a great read.

I definitely recommend it!

Contents

Chapter One

INTRODUCTION

There is perhaps no professional sports team in American history that had a more dedicated, deeply devoted group of followers than the Dodgers of the 1940s and 50s.

These beloved Brooklyn fans were bonded together by heartbreak.

Five times between 1941 and 1953, they ascended to the World Series, the grandest stage in all sports in the mid-20th century, and all five times they lost to the New York Yankees.

On three occasions in that stretch, they woke up knowing that a victory on this day over the Bronx Bombers would result in the Brooklyn Dodgers being World Champions. All three times, the Dodgers ended the day in disappointment.

In 1951, the Dodgers had another certain trip to meet the Yankees in the Fall Classic all wrapped up. But after holding a 13.5 game lead in August, the season came down to one final playoff game for the National League title against their cross-town rivals, the Giants. The Dodgers led 4 - 1 in the bottom of the 9th inning. The Giants scored a run and the Dodgers lead dwindled to 4 – 2.

Then with one out and two men on base, Bobby Thomson hit a line drive into the lower deck of the left field stands at the Polo Grounds, and Giants' radio broadcaster Russ Hodges repeatedly screamed into his microphone, ***"The Giants win the pennant!"*** The deliriously happy Hodges, and all Giants fans experienced a moment of elation that was unknown and unfathomable to their opponents faithful followers from Flatbush.

Roger Kahn, who published his masterpiece, "The Boys of Summer," in 1972, captured the core of why Brooklyn Dodgers fans adored 'dem Bums when he penned this line, ***"You may glory in a team triumphant, but you fall in love with a team in defeat."***

My dad Stanley is one of those who fell in love with the Brooklyn Dodgers. He was the perfect age to become indoctrinated as a Dodgers fan, six years old when they first played the Yankees in the World Series in 1941. And he was 18, when they lost to the Yankees for the fifth time in 1953.

My dad had never known the Dodgers bumbling days in the 1920s and 30s, when they routinely finished in the "second division," the lower tier of the National League, earning themselves the affectionate nickname, 'dem Bums.

No, in the years Stanley grew up he only knew the Dodgers as a perennial pennant contender, but never a World Series champion.

When I asked my dad recently what memory stands out most in all the years he followed the Brooklyn Dodgers growing up, he thought about it for just a few seconds and then he simply said, ***"Wait 'til next year."*** Then I informed him that phrase, which we have all heard before, is actually attributed to Brooklyn Dodgers fans of his era. It's a fact. You can Google it.

Of course, Stanley, and all of those Brooklyn Dodgers fans, experienced the ultimate sports heartbreak after the 1957 season. That year they didn't lose the World Series. They had finished the season 8 games back of the Braves. Losing wasn't the problem. No, the Dodgers did the unthinkable. They ended their ties to Brooklyn and moved the team to Los Angeles. Stanley was so distraught that he stopped following baseball altogether for many years.

I wrote this book because I wanted to understand what the experience was like being a Brooklyn Dodgers fan. And I also wanted to enable my dad to re-visit some of the experience of what it was to be a Dodgers fan before they abandoned him in 1957.

So as The Sports Time Traveler, I went back in time, virtually, to experience an entire season of the Brooklyn Dodgers.

In 2025, I set my sports time travel machine dial back precisely 70 years to 1955. And I followed 'dem Bums one-day-at-a-time.

The year 1955 was the perfect time for me to go back and experience the Dodgers for several reasons. That year was the first summer of my dad's life that he didn't have access to follow the Dodgers, so it was a year I could help him follow that he had not already experienced.

My dad was a rising junior in college at Temple University in Philadelphia, attending the summer term in that year of 1955. And in those days, if you didn't live in the city of the team you were rooting for, you couldn't exactly follow them too closely. There was, of course, no internet. And radio and TV broadcasts in Philadelphia were limited to following the Phillies. The Philadelphia Inquirer newspaper had just brief wire stories of Dodgers games. And the Philadelphia Daily News didn't cover Dodgers games at all.

In addition, by going back to 1955, it provided me with the proper perspective to understand this Brooklyn Dodgers team. They had already suffered those five World Series losses to the Yankees, as well as the gut punch, "the shot heard round the world," pennant loss to the Giants, in addition to another lost pennant to the "Whiz Kids," the 1950 Philadelphia Phillies, on the final day of that season.

And by 1955 the Dodgers' core group, those "Boys of Summer," had been together for a remarkably long time for a baseball team. The key players in the lineup had remained exactly the same.

On opening day 1949, the lineup included:

Pee Wee Reese
Jackie Robinson
Duke Snider
Roy Campanella
Gil Hodges
Carl Furillo

On opening day 1955, the lineup included:

Pee Wee Reese
Jackie Robinson
Duke Snider
Roy Campanella
Gil Hodges
Carl Furillo

Those same 6 players were beginning their 7th consecutive season in the starting lineup. There likely has never been another baseball team, at any level, that ever had the same core group together, all playing at the highest level in baseball at their respective positions, for a longer stretch of time.

This was another factor that bonded Brooklyn fans to the Dodgers. The fans developed the deep emotional connection with the team that can only be formed when one is extremely familiar with the players. It's not the uniforms the players wear that drives the attraction to a team. It's the people in those uniforms. And for Brooklyn fans those people largely stayed the same year after year. The players forged the bond between Brooklyn fans and the ball club.

Kids emulated those players in sandlot fields and in stick ball games. At Ebbets Field you could see the players up close. You could possibly meet the players, and you could entertain dreams about what it would be like to be a Brooklyn Dodgers' player yourself.

One more element solidified the fans love of the team - their home. Ebbets Field, the place where the Brooklyn Dodgers had played their games since 1913, was a cozy little "band box" of a ballpark. It wasn't a humungous baseball cathedral like Yankee Stadium. And it wasn't an aging oddity of an arena like the Polo Grounds. Ebbets Field was perfect for baseball. All the fans were near the action. And it had a unique 40-foot barrier in right field. It consisted of a 20 foot concrete wall topped by a 20 foot wire screen. The concrete portion sloped inward towards the field in the lower 10 feet. The upper 10 feet were vertically straight up, but this created a crease at the mid-point.

The oddities of the right field wall gave the Dodgers a distinct home field advantage. Long time right fielder Carl Furillo became expert in how to play the caroms off the wall. And lefty-hitting Duke Snider specialized in sending spherical missile shots over the wall and onto Bedford Avenue and beyond.

Now that we're well into the digital age, with a constant barrage of daily distractions, in which loyalties are fragmented, and a myriad of media sources constantly compete for our attention, it's quite possible there will never be another team that engenders such adoration, such faithfulness as the Dodgers did in Brooklyn.

Now join me as I take you back in time to experience the 1955 season of the Brooklyn Dodgers. In my journey, I followed every single game of that year, one-day-at-a-time. But in this book I've only included stories from games in which there was something so exciting I had to share them with you.

Each chapter tells the story of one special game. The stories are based on my readings of multiple newspaper accounts of the games. When there were radio broadcasts available, I also listened to them. And I let you know where you can find those broadcasts. If you don't want to spend the time to listen to entire baseball games, I have provided time stamps of the key points in the games that caught my attention, along with descriptions of the action and sometimes quotes from the radio announcers calls of the game.

At the beginning of each chapter, the date indicated is the date I read the newspaper accounts of that particular game. This means the games themselves took place the prior day. I have adopted this style for The Sports Time Traveler so that I, or any reader, would know what day to go back to in finding the newspaper accounts.

Unlike traditional sports writing, I don't let you know the outcome of a game until the end of the chapter. In this way, you get to experience each of the games as if you were there. The drama builds throughout the chapter so that you can feel the same late inning tension that fans felt back in 1955. Similarly, I don't share the outcome of the season until the end of the book. Fans who know their history or choose to look it up on the internet can readily find out what happened to the 1955 Dodgers. But if you wish to have the full fan experience of following the 1955 Dodgers, I suggest you avoid the temptation to find out what happened until reading the end of the final chapter.

Now let's begin the journey together.

Chapter Two

The 1955 Dodgers Set a Major League Record

EBBETS FIELD - April 22, 1955

The Sports Time Traveler is following the Boys of Summer, the Brooklyn Dodgers, in their 1955 season.

And what a start it has been to the season. Going into yesterday's game, the Dodgers had tied the all-time major league record of 9 wins to begin the season.

Background

This Dodgers team has been sensational over the past decade. They've been to the World Series 4 times in the past 8 seasons. But *every single time* they lost to the Yankees, including in 1947, 1949, 1952, and 1953. Last year, they were in contention down the stretch for the NL pennant again. Following a 7 game winning streak in September, they were just 3 games behind the Giants on September

15th. Then 5 straight losses did them in, and they finished 2nd with a record of 92 - 62.

1955 Predictions

Going into this season, there was some concern that the Dodgers were getting too old. Sports columnist George Beahon of the Rochester Democrat & Chronicle picked the Dodgers to finish 4th in the 8 team league. Not including the war years, the Dodgers have been no worse than 3rd since 1938.

Beahon cited Roy Campanella's injured hand in 1954 as a major reason for expecting the decline of the Dodgers. Campy, a two-time MVP in 1951 and 1953, was only able to bat .207 last year. Now at 33 years old, could he rebound?

And other team leaders are perhaps on the backside of their careers. Shortstop Pee Wee Reese, the Dodgers' captain, is 36. Jackie Robinson is also 36. And Carl Furillo is 33.

In addition, 28-year-old Don Newcombe, a 20 game winner in 1951, had come back in 1954 from 2 years in the service and pitched poorly, winning just 9 games with an ERA of 4.55. Will Newk ever regain his form as the number one starter?

The Rival New York Giants

The cross-town Giants, behind with their young superstar, Willie Mays, the 23-year-old phenom and 1954 MVP, who led the Giants to a stunning sweep of the 111 win Cleveland Indians in the World Series, look poised to be the new kings of New York baseball.

It's not hard to see why some sportswriters think the Dodgers' time has come and gone with no World Series victory to show for it.

The 1955 Season Begins in Record Style

The Dodgers quickly proved otherwise as the season began last week. After beating the Pirates at home 6 - 1 on opening day, the Dodgers went to the Polo Grounds to face the World Champion Giants. They took the two games 10 - 8 and 6 - 3. They continued on the road to Pittsburgh, winning 3 at Forbes Field. Then on to Philadelphia, where they won 2 more before heading back home to Brooklyn.

Two days ago, they tied the modern-day record of 9 straight wins to begin the season in a 3 - 2 decision over the Phillies. They did it in somewhat dramatic fashion. Behind 2 - 0 with 2 outs in the bottom of the 7th, the Dodgers loaded the bases without getting a hit as Roy Campanella and George Shuba walked, and Jackie Robinson got hit by a pitch. Then Duke Snider walked to bring home the Dodgers' first run. Next up was Gil Hodges, who slashed a ground ball single into center, scoring 2 runs and putting the Dodgers ahead 3 - 2.

Relief pitcher Clem Labine shut out the Phillies in the 8th and 9th, allowing no hits, to pick up the save.

Going for 10 in a Row

Yesterday afternoon, the Dodgers took on the Phillies again at Ebbets Field in a 1:30pm game. The weather was dry and a touch chilly. It was 58 degrees to start the game, and the high hit 61. Really not a bad day to be at the ballpark to witness a possible record-setting 10th consecutive win.

Yet a disappointing crowd of just 3,874 paid customers showed up for the game.

After the game, Dodgers' Pee Wee Reese told Jack Lang in a special to the Staten Island Advance, ***"I don't know what's happened to the fans. It must be television."*** The game was broadcast live on channel 9.

Russ Meyer was on the mound for the Dodgers. Meyer has been a solid pitcher for the Dodgers the past 2 seasons going 26 - 11 with 4 shutouts in 60 starts. In Meyer's 1st start, a week earlier, he had thrown a 2-hit shutout.

Yesterday, Meyer lost his 2nd "shutout" bid when on the 2nd pitch of the game, Phillies' leadoff batter, Bobby Morgan, hit a home run on what New York Daily News writer, Dana Mozley, referred to as, ***"a gopher pitch."***

The Phillies sent perhaps the best starter in baseball over the past 5 years to the mound - Robin Roberts. Roberts has won 115 games in the past 5 seasons (23 per year), while keeping his ERA under 3.00. And, he'd picked up right where he left off in 1954, winning his first 2 starts and allowing just 2 earned runs in 20 innings pitched.

Roberts put down the Dodgers 1-2-3 in the bottom of the 1st.

But in the bottom of the 2nd, the Dodgers got 3 hits and 2 runs off Roberts and took a 2 - 1 lead.

In the top of the 3rd, after Russ Meyer gave up a single, double, walk and wild pitch, Walt Alston decided to take out his starter, who Mozley reported, ***"didn't have it"*** yesterday. Alston gave the ball to Joe Black, the star of the staff from 1952, but ***"a bust ever since,"*** according to Mozley.

Black proceeded to pitch a fine game, allowing just 5 hits and 2 runs over the next 6 and 2/3 innings.

Meanwhile, the Dodgers' batters feasted on the normally feisty Roberts. They pummeled him with 4 home runs in the 3rd through 5th innings, including a 3-run bomb by the Duke.

The Dodgers went on to win the game 14 - 4.

The victory made the Brooklyn Dodgers the first team in the modern era (since 1900) to win the first 10 games of the season. Only the 1884 New York National League team has ever won more games to start a season (12).

However, unlike the 1884 team, the Dodgers didn't get to play their first 21 games of the season at home. While the New York streak of 12 in 1884 was all done at home, the Dodgers have won 7 of their 10 games on the road.

The Dodgers' 10 wins have also been by a combined score of 70 - 31, an average of a 7 - 3 victory in each contest.

Here is the complete set of scores during the streak:

April 13 – Dodgers 6 Pirates 1 – winner Carl Erskine

April 14 – Dodgers 10 Giants 8 – winner Don Newcombe

April 15 – Dodgers 6 Giants 3 – winner Billy Loes

April 16 – Dodgers 6 Pirates 0 – winner Russ Meyer

April 17 – Dodgers 10 Pirates 3 – winner Johnny Podres

April 17 – Dodgers 3 Pirates 2 – winner Clem Labine

April 18 – Dodgers 5 Phillies 2 – winner Carl Erskine

April 19 – Dodgers 7 Phillies 6 – winner Don Newcombe

April 20 – Dodgers 3 Phillies 2 – winner Billy Loes

April 21 – Dodgers 14 Phillies 4 – winner Joe Black

The Celebration

In the Dodgers' clubhouse after the game, New York Times reporter Roscoe McGowen noted there was a sign on the blackboard that read, ***"The Bums dood it, 10 straight."*** He also observed an odd celebration as, ***"the boys broke two phonograph records on Zimmer's head."*** That's utility infielder, Don Zimmer, who started in place of Reese at shortstop and had one of the homers. Zimmer went 4-for-4 on the day.

The Boys are Back in Town!

The 1955 Dodgers seem to be back in business in Brooklyn.

In addition to the pitchers allowing just 3 runs per game, the batters are collectively hitting .345.

Here are the averages of the Dodgers' batters that have at least 15 at bats through 10 games:

.385 Carl Furillo
.361 Duke Snider
.333 Don Zimmer
.314 Roy Campanella
.297 Gil Hodges
.289 Jackie Robinson
.263 Sandy Amoros
.244 Jim Gilliam
.160 Pee Wee Reese

Continuing Coverage of the 1955 Dodgers

The Sports Time Traveler will continue following the Dodgers day-by-day in 1955 and report to you whenever there is something so compelling I just have to come back to the present and share it.

NOTE from the present time

The Dodgers' record of 10 consecutive wins to start the season stood for 26 years until it was surpassed by the 1981 Oakland A's.

A year after the A's big start, the Braves won the current record of 13 straight to start the 1982 season. That record was tied by the 1987 Brewers and the 2023 Rays.

But none of the teams that surpassed the Dodgers' streak ever had to face the defending World Series champions. The Dodgers beat the 1954 World Series champion Giants in the 2nd and 3rd games of the season.

Chapter Three

A Crazy April Day at Ebbets Field

The game on April 24, 1955 has to qualify as one of the zaniest ever at Ebbets

EBBETS FIELD - Monday, April 25, 1955

The Sports Time Traveler is following the 1955 Brooklyn Dodgers day-by-day precisely 70 years in the past.

I'm only posting stories when there is something so compelling I just have to share it.

Yesterday's game qualifies.

After winning their first 10 games of the season to set a major league record, the Dodgers finally lost to the Giants on Friday when they squandered a 3 - 0 lead in the 8th inning and lost 5 - 4. They came back to win again Saturday to boost their record to 11 - 1.

Yesterday's game started at Ebbets Field at 2pm on a cold Sunday afternoon for the 21,615 fans at the park. The temperature was just 48 degrees for the opening pitch. It never got above 49 during the game.

The Dodgers sent Don Newcombe to the mound for the 3rd time so far in the young season. Newk is still a big question mark. After winning 20 in 1951, he spent 1952 and 1953 in the service, and last season he was a shell of his former self. He's only 28, so big things are still expected from him. He did win his first 2 starts, but his ERA in those 2 games was an un-Newk like 5.79. He benefitted from the big Brooklyn bats piling up runs.

Yesterday, facing the Giants, Newk started out rocky. The Giants were hitting the ball hard, but he had managed to ***"escape damage,"*** according to Dick Young in the New York Daily News. Newk managed to get the first 8 Giants out before giving up a line drive single to center by Giants' pitcher, Don Liddle.

Newk maintained a shutout through 3 innings, and a Pee Wee Reese homer in the 3rd gave the Dodgers a 1 - 0 lead.

In the top of the 4th, with one out and a man on 1st, Willie Mays came to the plate. The 23-year-old phenom blasted one into the upper deck in left field. It was the Say Hey Kid's 1st homer of the 1955 season, here in the Giants' 10th game. And it put the Giants in front 2 - 1.

The Dodgers came back in the bottom of the 4th. Carl Furillo led off with his major league leading 6th home run of the season.

With the score now tied at 2 and Newk getting hit hard, manager Walt Alston decided to pinch hit for him. After the game Newk indicated that his arm had grown stiff. Pinch hitter Frank Kellert walked and a few batters later, Duke Snider's line drive to right scored Kellert and Jim Gilliam and put the Dodgers ahead 4 - 2.

The Dodgers remained in front despite Willie Mays's 2nd homer of the game in the 6th. And going into the 8th inning it was 5 - 3 Dodgers. Don Hoak led off the bottom of the 8th with a triple for the Dodgers. After pitcher Billy Loes struck out, Jim Gilliam hit a ball to deep center field. Jack Lang in the Staten Island Advance described the play, ***"Mays went back and then came in for the catch and fired a strike to the plate. His throw caught Hoak, one of the team's fastest runners, to complete an inning-ending double play."***

It was a sensational throw by the Say Hey Kid. Jim Ogle in the Newark Star-Ledger called the play by Mays, ***"one of his patented throws."***

Going into the top of the 9th with a 5 - 3 lead, Dodgers' pitcher Billy Loes was in line to get the save. With one down Whitey Lockman hit a ground ball back to Loes. Dick Young reporting for the New York Daily News described what happened next, ***"Loes bobbled Lockman's comeback squib to the box and threw it wild past first - and threw up a gopher to Dark a moment later. Al tucked it into the left seats for his first homer - and a 5 - 5 game.***

The game stayed tied at 5 going into the bottom half of the 9th. Pee Wee Reese led off with a single to center. Duke Snider tried to bunt Reese over but popped it up for the 1st out. Then Gil Hodges struck out swinging. Next up was Sandy Amoros. He walked and now Reese, representing the potential winning run, was on 2nd base for Roy Campanella. Campy who had a terrible year battling a hand injury in 1954 and hit only .207, came into yesterday's game hitting .366. But Campy flew out to left and the game went into extra innings.

Willie Mays led off the 10th against Billy Loes with a single. On the next play, Monte Irvin hit a short fly to right center. Jack Lang writing for the Staten Island Advance described the action, ***"Duke Snider had the ball in his glove but Furillo crashed into him and the ball dropped for a base hit."***

After Billy Gardner bunted the runners over to 2nd and 3rd, the Giants' 3rd string catcher, Ray Katt came to the plate. Dick Young questioned Alston's strategy with Katt batting and the pitcher due up next, ***"With first open and no pinch hitters left on the Giant bench, the Brooks, for some strange reason, pitched to Katt. Ray blasted into the left stands, and the Giants led 8 - 5."***

It got worse.

The next 2 batters, Jim Hearn and Whitey Lockman, hit a single and a double. Now Alston took Loes out of the game and went to Ed Roebuck. But Roebuck got rocked right away. Al Dark singled to score Hearn. And Don Mueller singled to drive in Lockman with Al Dark moving to 3rd.

Then came the most bizarre play of the game. Hank Thompson lifted a fly to right field. Carl Furillo caught the ball for the 2nd out. And then Furillo ***"trotted for the bench,"*** according to Dick Young. Furillo thought the terrifying top of the 10th had been terminated. But the catch was just the 2nd out. And Al Dark tagged up and scored the 11th Giants' run uncontested. Giants' 1st base coach Freddie Fitzsimmons then told Don Mueller to break for 2nd base. Furillo apparently threw the ball to 2nd base resulting in a strange double play to end the misery.

It was now 11 - 5 Giants.

Of course, the home team got one more chance in the bottom of the 10th. Carl Furillo tried to make up for his gaffes in the field by leading off with a single. Don Hoak also singled. Then George Shuba struck out.

With 2 on and 1 down, Jim Gilliam singled to drive in Furillo. It was now 11 - 6 Giants.

Pee Wee Reese walked and the bases were loaded with 1 out.

This prompted Giants' manager Leo Durocher to change pitchers and bring in Johnny Antonelli. He promptly walked Duke Snider and now the score was 11 - 7 with the bases still loaded.

Antonelli next got Gil Hodges to strike out for out number 2.

But the Dodgers still had the bases loaded.

Next, Sandy Amoros singled driving in 2 runs to make it 11 - 9.

And when Roy Campenella singled, driving in Duke Snider, it was 11 - 10 Giants.

With 2 outs and the tying run on 2nd base, Carl Furillo was up again. Leo Durocher brought in Ruben Gomez to pitch to Furillo. While the pitching change was made, Walter Alston brought in rookie Bert Hamric to pinch run for Roy Campanella. Hamric represented the potential winning run. Bert Hamric was a 27-year-old contender for the left field position. He had played 726 games in the the Dodgers' minor league system, and last year, in 1954, had hit .341 in AAA ball in Montreal and St. Paul. And Hamric had demonstrated speed in the minors stealing as many as 32 bases in a single season.

Now with Carl Furillo batting, Bert Hamric, standing on 1st base, had to be thinking about the glory of scoring a winning run in his very 1st game, should Furillo hit one in the gap.

Furillo did indeed get wood on a pitch, but he ***"lifted a pop foul to the back of third. Henry Thompson collected it for the final out and the struggle was over,"*** according to John Drebinger in the New York Times.

The final score was Giants 11 - Dodgers 10.

The Giants improved to 4 - 6 on the season. The Dodgers dropped to 11 - 2.

Jack Lang made this observation after the game, ***"The Dodger victory string might be 13 today if... the Dodgers hadn't thrown the ball away. Friday night the Giants won, 5 - 4, with the winning run coming home on Don Zimmer's throwing error. Yesterday, the Giants were able to send the game into extra innings because Billy Loes threw an easy ground ball away just before Al Dark hit a game-tying homer in the ninth."***

So the 1955 Brooklyn Dodgers could easily have been standing today at 13 - 0.

The Sports Time Traveler will continue following the 1955 Brooklyn Dodgers and reporting when there is something so compelling I have to share it.

Chapter Four

The Boys of Summer Have a Curfew

EBBETS FIELD - May 3, 1955

Last night's game between the Brooklyn Dodgers and the Milwaukee Braves started at 8pm. When the schedule was set, the Dodgers and Braves agreed that the game would be played at night under the stipulation there would be an 11:15pm curfew. This would ensure that the Braves could catch their 12:30am train to Pittsburgh where they're scheduled to play tonight.

Sportswriters and fans only found out about the curfew as the game was about to get underway last night. Jack Lang wrote in the Staten Island Advance today, ***"The first knowledge the fans had of this was just before the game. It was announced over the P.A. system that no inning would start after 11:15. But they had already paid to get in. It was news to them - and to the press, who were also uninformed - that a curfew had been set."***

Dick Young shared his frustration with Dodgers' management over the secret curfew agreement in his article in the New York Daily News, ***"By mutual agreement of whom? ... the fans? They had been told only after they had bought their tickets and were in the park.***

It really shouldn't have been a problem, however. In the entire 1954 season, only 3 Dodgers' home games lasted more than 3 hours and 15 minutes.

Well, wouldn't you know it? Last night's game went into extra innings with the score nothing-to-nothing.

Carl Erskine of the Dodgers had allowed no runs and just 4 hits.

Gene Conley of the Braves was even better. In fact he was sensational. Conley had allowed no runs and only 2 ground ball hits by the pitcher, Erskine. Conley had no-hit the Dodgers' position players through 9 innings.

In the 10th inning, both starters remained in the game and had easy innings. Conley didn't give up a hit. Erskine let up a single, just the 5th Braves hit of the game, but stranded the runner on 1st.

The game continued on to the 11th.

After getting the first two batters out, Erskine gave up a double to Henry Aaron. The Dodgers elected to walk Eddie Mathews to enable a force out at 3rd base.

Next up was a batter that must strike fear into the hearts of all Dodgers' fans. It was Bobby Thomson, the man who won the 1951 pennant for the Giants with his famous shot heard round the world. Erskine walked Thomson to load the bases.

Next up was the dangerous Joe Adcock. Adcock hit a fly ball to deep right center. But Sandy Amoros was able to get to the ball to retire the side.

Conley got the Dodgers out quietly again in the bottom of the 11th. Roy Campanella did get a single with 2 outs, making that the 1st hit off Conley by a Dodger's position player. But Conley got the next batter, Sandy Amoros, to pop up to the catcher, and the game continued to the 12th.

The 12th Inning

Carl Erskine again came out to pitch the top of the 12th. He walked the first 2 batters. And they advanced to 2nd and 3rd base on a sacrifice bunt. Incredibly, the Braves elected to send Conley to bat with 1 out in the 12th. Conley was just a .156 batter last year. Conley grounded out, and the runners had to hold.

Now, Erskine had to face the leadoff batter, Bill Bruton. Bruton already had 2 of the Braves' 6 hits in the game. But Erskine got Bruton to hit a fly to left that was caught by Sandy Amoros, who had been moved to left field.

11:06 pm

Going into the bottom of the 12th there was a problem. It was now 11:06pm. If the Dodgers did not score, then the game was going to be called on account of the curfew and would go in the books as a tie.

Gene Conley came back out to the mound.

First up was Gil Hodges. He struck out swinging.

Next was Jackie Robinson. He walked.

11:09 pm

Now, Carl Furillo came to the plate. Furillo, who was leading the major leagues in home runs with 7, was 0 for 3 with a walk.

The first pitch to Furillo was a ball.

The second pitch was a hanging curve ball. Furillo swung. Dick Young described what happened as he referred to Furillo by his nickname, ***"Skoonj drove deep into the lower deck."***

Carl Furillo had hit a 2-run homer over the left field wall.

The Dodgers had won the game, 2 - 0 at 11:13pm.

Not only had Furillo won the game for the Dodgers just prior to the curfew, he had saved Ebbets Field according to Dick Young, ***"If Furillo hadn't homered, and the dramatic duel between Carl Erskine and Gene Conley had ended in empty nothingness, the few paying fans the Dodgers have left would have been justified in burning down Ebbets Field."***

Jack Lang similarly reported on the magnitude of Furillo's game-winning blast, ***"What might have happened if the 19,976 fans had been robbed of seeing this brilliant game played to a conclusion is hard to say. Suffice to say the Brooklyn club is deeply indebted to Furillo for ending it and saving them the embarrassment of explaining to fans why a curfew was set in the first place."***

While the Braves left quickly for their train to Pittsburgh, Jack Lang was able to interview the other hero of the game, pitcher Carl Erskine. Erskine had just pitched a 12 inning, 6-hit shutout. He told Lang that he ranked this game as the 3rd or 4th best of his career. His #1 was his record 14-strikeout game in the 1953 World Series. And his #2 was his no-hitter against the Cubs in 1952. This game he considered on par with his 1 - 0 victory in 10 innings over Warren Spahn in 1951.

The 1955 Brooklyn Dodgers now have a record of 16 - 2.

The Sports Time Traveler will continue to follow the 1955 Brooklyn Dodgers and share stories when there is something so exciting I have to write about it.

SPECIAL NOTE From The Sports Time Traveler

Another interesting footnote about the game is that there were no substitutions by either team in the entire 12 inning game. I checked with the Society for American Baseball Research, and the Director of Editorial Content, Jacob Pomrenke, confirmed that this is the longest game by time (3 hours and 13 minutes) in the live ball era (since 1920) in which there were NO substitutions. All 18 players that started the game were still in the game at its conclusion. This is one of many fascinating discoveries I've made in following the 1955 Brooklyn Dodgers through the newspaper archives.

Chapter Five

Is Newk Back?

WRIGLEY FIELD - May 11, 1955

Before the Korean War, Don Newcombe was the Dodgers' top starter. In the 3 seasons from 1949 - 1951, Newk won 56 games and had 12 shutouts.

Then Newk missed the entire seasons of 1952 and 1953, serving in the military.

Newk's being drafted likely cost the Dodgers at least one World Series championship. The Yankees beat the Dodgers in 7 games in 1952 and 6 games in 1953. But the Yankees core starters of Eddie Lopat, Vic Raschi, and Allie Reynolds played in both of those World Series, while Newcombe was serving in Korea.

When Newk came back in 1954, he was a shell of himself on the mound. He was 9 - 8 with an ERA of 4.55. He had never pitched so poorly.

At 28 years old, Newk came into this season as a big question mark. Yet, his age would suggest he should be in his prime. What contribution would Newk make to the 1955 Dodgers?

Coming into yesterday afternoon's game in Chicago, Newk was still a question mark. Yes, he had won all 3 starts he had made so far this season. But that's very deceptive. Newk's ERA in those 3 starts was 5.50. And in his last start, he had to come out after 4 innings with arm stiffness. The Dodgers had to be wondering if the old Newk would ever be back.

Last week Newk got into a dispute with the Dodgers. Since Newk was being held out of games to let his stiff arm improve, he was asked to pitch batting practice. Newk took this as an insult and refused, which resulted in a suspension. The suspension was short-lived and everything was smoothed over, but it had to add to the question marks around whether the old Newk will ever be seen again.

Yesterday, the Dodgers sent Newk back to the mound to start for the first time in over 2 weeks. For this Tuesday afternoon game, only 6,686 fans showed up in Wrigley Field. In New York, the game was not on TV, and it was not on the radio. Newk had never lost to the Cubs. So, perhaps this might be a nice quiet place for Newk to begin again.

Newk got off to a good start, putting down the Cubs in order in the first 3 innings. Since the Cubs came into the game with the most runs scored of any team in the National League besides the 1st place Dodgers, this was a good sign for Newk.

In those first 3 frames, the Dodgers managed just 1 hit and the score was knotted at 0 - 0.

In the bottom of the 4th, Cubs' 2nd baseman Gene Baker wrapped a line drive single up the middle, right past Newk's head according to Roscoe McGowen of the New York Times, breaking up Newk's chances for a no-hitter.

A moment later, Roy Campanella threw out Baker trying to steal 2nd. According to Newsday, Campy's throw was so strong that 2nd baseman Junior Gilliam had the ball before Baker even went into his slide. And when Eddie Miksis struck out, Newk was out of the inning having faced only 3 batters.

In the top of the 5th, Newk came up and got a single himself, but was stranded at 1st and the game remained 0 - 0.

Newk had yet another 1- 2- 3 inning in the 5th, closing out the inning when the 2nd year shortstop Ernie Banks hit a fly ball to Sandy Amoros in right field. Banks was 2nd in the Rookie-of-the-Year voting last season and in 1953 he batted .347 for the Kansas City Monarchs in the Negro Leagues.

NOTE from The Sports Time Traveler

Ernie Banks stats from the Negro Leagues sadly do not count as part of his MLB stats because MLB has arbitrarily decided that all Negro League stats after 1948 do not count.

This has cost Ernie Banks 19 home runs. Those 19 home runs would put Banks in the top 20 all-time with 531. And, he would stay in the top 20 for some time to come, as no active player is within 100 home runs of that mark.

Now back to 1955.

In the top of the 6th, the Dodgers finally got on the board. Duke Snider smacked a line drive deep into the right field seats. It was the Duke's 9th homer and 30th RBI in just 24 games this year. Duke leads the National League in both departments. It was also Snider's 200th career HR. Dick Young of the New York Daily News described it, ***"It was a hummer off Warren Hacker, and it had to cut through a stiff cross-wind whipping in from left."***

In the bottom of the 6th, 7th and 8th innings Newk continued mowing down the Cubs 1 - 2 - 3 in each frame.

The Dodgers manufactured 2 more runs. In the 7th, Newk got another single and Jim Gilliam hit a sacrifice fly. And in the top of the 9th, Pee Wee Reese drove in Jim Gilliam.

The Dodgers led 3 - 0 when Newk took the mound in the bottom of the 9th. Newk had not had a shutout since 1951. And, the Cubs had the bottom of the order coming to the plate.

The first batter was a pinch hitter, Jim King. King, a rookie, was making the 10th plate appearance of his career. He had yet to get a hit. He didn't get it on this at bat either as he grounded to Gilliam at 2nd.

Next up was the catcher, Harry Chiti. Chiti, like Newk, had missed 2 years in Korea. But he had missed 1953 and 1954, and this was just his 26th game back in the majors, although he was batting an acceptable .250. Chiti hit a grounder to Pee Wee Reese who tossed it to Gil Hodges at 1st for out number 2.

Next up was another pinch hitter, Frank Baumholtz. The 36-year-old has batted over .300 over across the past 3 years. He lofted a fly ball to Sandy Amoros, who had been moved to play left field by manager Walter Alston. Amoros caught it, and the game went into the books.

Don Newcombe had pitched a 1 hit shutout. It was a 96-pitch masterpiece.

The outfield only had 5 balls hit to them, ***"none of them difficult,"*** according to Edward Prell in the Chicago Tribune.

Newk had faced just the minimum 27 batters.

McGowen in the New York Times wrote about the minimum 27 batters faced by Don Newcombe, ***"Although no official records are kept on the subject of pitchers facing only twenty-seven men, the belief is that such an achievement is even rarer than a no-hitter. For example, Bob Feller, who has fashioned three no-hitters and twelve one-hitters for the Cleveland Indians, never has faced fewer than twenty-nine batters in a game."***

Newk was very close to having pitched a perfect game. There has not been a perfect game in MLB since Charley Robertson of the White Sox threw one in 1922.

Roscoe McGowen of the New York Times called it Newk's ***"finest hour."***

Dick Young of the New York Daily News called it, ***"the finest game of Newk's career."***

Young also had harsh words for Dodgers' owner Walter O'Malley. O'Malley was still talking about how much Newk would be fined for his refusal to pitch batting practice that led to his suspension. O'Malley had said, ***"Anywhere from $250 to $500. It depends on how I feel."*** Young suggested, ***"If you meant how you'd feel about Newk, you should feel pretty high right now. Almost high enough to say: 'Forget it.'"***

By the way, with the shutout, Newk has still never lost to the Cubs. He's 11 - 0 in his career.

In the Chicago Tribune today, there was a big picture of Don Newcombe and Roy Campanella giving the game ball to manager Walter Alston as a 25th wedding anniversary present.

The Dodgers are now an incredible 22 - 2 on the season. They have a 9.5 game lead already on the defending World Series champion New York Giants.

The 22 - 2 start is the best in major league history.

The Sports Time Traveler will continue to follow the 1955 Dodgers.

Chapter Six

The Best 54 Game Start

EBBETS FIELD, BROOKLYN - June 12, 1955

The Sports Time Traveler is following the 1955 Brooklyn Dodgers day-by-day.

It's been an incredible start to the season here in 1955 for this Dodgers' team that was viewed as "over the hill" by baseball experts. The Dodgers have never won a World Series, and they recently lost the World Series to the Yankees in 1947, 1949, 1952 and 1953. They also lost heartbreaking close pennant races in 1950 and 1951.

Their time to win it all had seemed to close last year in 1954, when they finished 5 games behind the New York Giants who were led by their emerging superstar Willie Mays.

But lo and behold the Dodgers this year raced out to a 22 - 2 start at the beginning of this year. After a mediocre 6 - 8 stretch, they've now piled on 14 wins in their last 16 games.

That puts their record as of this morning at 42 - 12.

NOTE from the present time

I interrupt this article to inform you that the 1955 Brooklyn Dodgers record of 42 - 12 is something special. In the past 70 years, no team has had a better 54 game start than the 1955 Brooklyn Dodgers.

Now back to 1955

Newking 'Em

There are many players responsible for the Dodgers' remarkable success this year. Perhaps none more than the resurgence of starting pitcher Don Newcombe. Newcombe, the Dodgers ace starter in 1949 - 1951, was a big question mark coming into this season. He had not been the same since missing the entire 1952 and 1953 seasons in the military. But Newcombe has been perfect this year. This week he raised his record to a perfect 10 - 0, making him one of the only starting pitchers ever to achieve that mark.

Newcombe is pitching so efficiently that he needed just 91 pitches to beat the Reds in his last outing.

Newcombe is also having a sensational season at the plate. He's batting .400 with 4 home runs. In the victory over the Reds this week, Newk singled and scored the Dodgers' first run. Then later he doubled to drive in a run. Newk pretty much beat the Reds all by himself as he was directly responsible for 2 of the 3 Dodgers' runs, while holding Cincinnati to a single run on a ball that was crushed by Ted Kluszewski.

Joseph Sheehan in the New York Times pointed out that, ***"Not many ball players reach this stage of the season with a pitching percentage of 1.000 and a batting average of .400."***

It's very likely no one else has ever done that.

Campy is Crushing It!

Another major reason for the Dodgers' brilliant start is the return of catcher Roy Campanella to MVP-like play. After winning the MVP in 1951 and 1953, last year Campy battled a season long hand injury, and hit a career low .207. At 33 years old, many felt Campy might never regain his form. But Campy, who hit home runs in each of the past 2 games, now has an MVP worthy batting line:

19 HRs (1st in NL)
58 RBIs (2nd in NL)
.332 Avg. (3rd in NL)

The Duke

If you noticed that Campy is 2nd in the NL in RBIs, it's because Dodgers' centerfielder, Duke Snider is 1st. The Duke has 60 RBIs through 54 games. Snider's batting line looks similar to Campy's.

And Duke has made many fine catches in centerfield as well. He's currently outpacing his fellow centerfielders in New York in every category.

Take a look at this comparison between Willie, Mickey and the Duke:

HRs	RBIs	Average	
16	39	.296	Willie Mays
14	41	.311	Mickey Mantle
18	60	.316	Duke Snider

Starting Pitching

Another piece of the puzzle for the 1955 Dodgers has been the other 3 starters in the 4 man rotation besides Newcombe. Carl Erskine, Billy Loes and Johnny Podres have given 2nd year manager Walt Alston consistent quality starts. Just take a look at the last 4 outings of the quartet:

Podres threw a 5 hit shutout to improve his record to 6 - 3.

Newcombe pitched a 4 hit complete game victory to get to 10 - 0.

Erskine fired a 4 hit shutout to boost his record to 8 - 2.

Loes tossed a complete game 5 hitter to get to 7 - 2.

Mysteriously Missing

There's one thing that is absent from all of this - the fans.

Ebbets Field has been incredibly empty on weekdays. This past Tuesday afternoon's game had paid attendance of just 4,481.

And there has not been a single sellout on the weekends all season.

Regarding the poor fan support, the June 1st New York Daily News had this note about a comment made by the Dodgers' owner, ***"Walter O'Malley drops subtle hints aimed at consumer complacency, 'There's a very important election being held in Los Angeles. It's on a bond issue for the purpose of spending 4.5 million dollars on a ballpark to seat 63,000.'"***

The Sports Time Traveler will continue following the 1955 Dodgers and report to you when there is something so compelling I just have to share it.

Chapter Seven

Koufax's Debut

19-Year-Old Sandy Koufax Pitches in His First Professional Baseball Game

MILWAUKEE COUNTY STADIUM - June 25, 1955

The Sports Time Traveler has been following the 1955 Dodgers day-by-day since spring training.

Yesterday was a real treat. I got to experience the very first professional outing of Sandy Koufax.

Koufax was signed to a $20,000 "bonus baby" contract by the Dodgers last year. Under baseball rules in 1955, if you give a player such a large signing bonus they must be on the major league roster.

As a result, Koufax has not played a single game in the minor leagues. He has just sat on the Dodgers' bench all season watching every game. It must have been fun at least for Koufax to watch. He is after all the only Dodgers' player who was actually born in Brooklyn. And Sandy got to see the team get off to the hottest start of any ball club in the past 70 years. They are now in first place with a record of 49 - 17, and 13 games in front of the Braves and the Cubs. The defending World Series champion New York Giants are 16 games back.

Yesterday, with the Dodgers down 7 - 1 going into the bottom of the 5th inning, Dodgers' manager Walt Alston decided it was finally time to ***"take the***

wraps off Sandy Koufax," as The New York Times beat writer John Drebinger wrote.

The 19-year-old Koufax, who has only previously pitched in little league and for the University of Cincinnati, promptly gave up a single to the first batter he faced, Johnny Logan. Next up was Eddie Mathews, one of the top home run hitters in baseball the past 2 seasons with 47 in 1953 and 40 in 1954. Earlier in the game, Mathews hit his 16th homer of this season off one of the Dodgers' ace pitchers, Carl Erksine. Mathews hit a grounder to Koufax. It was a perfect double play ball, but Koufax threw the ball into center field, and suddenly there were Braves' runners on 2nd and 3rd.

Up next came one of the best young hitters in baseball, 21-year-old Henry Aaron. Aaron had hit his 12th homer of the season earlier in the game off Erskine, knocking Carl out of the game. And Aaron is now batting .327, 6th best in the National League. Koufax walked Aaron to load the bases.

Next up was the man that likely still gives Dodgers fans shudders when they hear his name. And I don't just mean in 1955, I mean in the present time in the mid-2020s. It was Bobby Thomson - the man who hit the "shot heard round the world," in 1951, that cost the Dodgers the pennant and crushed Dodgers fans.

Thomson had been traded to the Braves by the Giants in 1954. Officially the trade was made to shore up the Giants' pitching staff. But I wonder if the Giants were also shipping out Thomson out of pity for their cross-town rivals who would no longer have to see his dreaded name daily each season in the New York papers.

Koufax struck out Thomson.

That strikeout was of no solace to anyone rooting for the Dodgers in this lopsided game.

But for Koufax, who lived in Brooklyn when Thomson hit the infamous 1951 home run that broke the hearts of Dodgers' fans, it must have been a thrill to fan the man who has given Dodgers' supporters nightmares ever since.

And that's how Sandy Koufax recorded the first strikeout of his major league career.

He still however had the bases loaded and just 1 out. Next to the plate was the fearsome Joe Adcock. Adcock had been 8th in the MVP voting in 1954. Koufax got Adcock to hit a grounder to Pee Wee Reese at shortstop. It was another double play ball. Unlike Koufax earlier, Reese made the throw on target to Jim Gilliam at 2nd base. Gilliam turned and threw to Gil Hodges at 1st base, and Koufax had gotten out of the inning without a run scoring.

In the 6th inning, Koufax faced the bottom of the Braves' order. He got the first 2 batters out on a grounder and a fly to center. Then up came the Braves' pitcher Lew Burdette. He got him looking at a called 3rd strike. It was a 1-2-3 inning for Koufax, the first one of his career.

In the top of the 7th, Koufax came out of the game for a pinch hitter, and thus his first game was done. Koufax had given up no runs and 1 hit in 2 innings of work.

The Dodgers lost the game 8 - 2, but still have a commanding lead in the National League.

Jack Lang in the Staten Island Advance wrote about Koufax's brief appearance, ***"Koufax, nervous at the start pitched well in his major league debut."***

John Craig of the Newark Star-Ledger also wrote a short bit on Koufax's first game, ***"KOUFAX USED - With their bullpen ranks worn thin, bonus boy Sandy Koufax was given his major league baptism."***

NOTE from The Sports Time Traveler

As a virtual time traveler from the future, I was sort of hoping, maybe even expecting to find a prescient sportswriter on June 25, 1955, make mention that this looks like the start of a possible Hall of Fame career.

But no one wrote that.

I would however, like to share with you the story of how Koufax came to be a Dodger.

At age 18, in the summer of 1954, he was invited to a workout at Ebbets Field by Dodgers' scout Al Campanis.

Campanis had received a tip from the youth sports columnist of the Brooklyn Eagle newspaper, Jimmy Murphy. Murphy had seen Koufax pitch in sandlot games after he came home from a successful freshman baseball season at the University of Cincinnati where he had been a walk on pitcher after basketball season was over (Koufax was attending the university on a basketball scholarship).

Murphy told Campanis that Koufax had a *"legendary fastball."*

Campanis described the tryout 25 years later in a January 28, 1979 article in the New York Times,

"As soon as I saw that fastball, the hair raised up on my arms. The only other time the hair on my arms raised up was in Rome when I saw Michelangelo's paintings on the ceiling of the Sistine chapel."

CHAPTER EIGHT

Sandy's First Start

THE NOT SO SOON TO BE GREAT KOUFAX STARTED HIS FIRST GAME ON JULY 6, 1955

FORBES FIELD, PITTSBURGH - July 7, 1955

The Sports Time Traveler is following the 1955 Dodgers. Yesterday, they had a twilight doubleheader at Forbes Field against the last place Pittsburgh Pirates.

The Dodgers came into the day in 1st place in the National League, 12 games in front of the Cubs, and 17 games ahead of the defending World Series champion Giants.

The Dodgers sport a gaudy 55 - 23 record. That puts them on pace to equal the 110 wins record of the 1927 Murderer's Row Yankees. And would put them on track for the major league mark of 116 wins if they were playing a 162 game schedule, but here in 1954 the season has just 154 games.

In the 1st game of the twin bill, Dodgers' starter Carl Erskine had a 4 -1 lead and 2 outs in the 6th inning when he set a major league record of the wrong kind. Erskine gave up consecutive homers to Jerry Lynch, Frank Thomas and Dale Long.

Despite the hammering in the 6th, Erskine found himself with a 7 - 4 lead going into the last of the 8th. The first 2 Pirates' batters drilled a double and a single and the tying run was now at the plate.

Dodgers' manager Walt Alston decided it was finally time to take Erskine out. He went to his bullpen for Ed Roebuck. The 23-year-old Roebuck is a brilliant rookie reliever. He came into the game with a 2.26 ERA in 30 games.

Roebuck has been pitching in the Dodgers' organization for 7 seasons, since he was just 17 years old. He had pitched 237 games in the minor leagues prior to this year. In the past 4 seasons in the minors, he had started 99 games with 14 of them resulting in shutouts.

Roebuck got out of the jam, allowing just 1 run to score on a groundout. In the 9th, he allowed just 1 single to Dick Groat and the game ended when Roebuck got another rookie, Roberto Clemente to ground out.

The Dodgers had their 56th win.

The Dodgers' Starter for Game 2

19-year-old rookie, Sandy Koufax was the starting pitcher in the nightcap yesterday. Koufax is what is known here in 1955 as a bonus baby. He was given a bonus of about $20,000 to sign with the Dodgers before the season. And under baseball rules at this time, players who are given large bonuses must be kept on the major league roster. Sandy Koufax was a Brooklyn Dodger without ever having played a single game in the minors.

Until yesterday, Koufax had not yet started a game with the Dodgers. In fact, Koufax had never started a regular season game in professional baseball.

The last time Sandy Koufax was the starting pitcher in a baseball game was in the preseason when he faced the Dodgers' B team for 2 innings of work on March 18th in Vero Beach. In those 2 innings no batter put a ball in play. Koufax got 5Ks, and his 6th out came when a man he had walked earlier was doubled up after a strikeout.

Prior to that start, Koufax had started 4 games in the spring of 1954 for the University of Cincinnati Bearcats freshman team. That's right, the freshman team. Sandy Koufax never even played in a varsity game in college.

That's a total of 5 games that Koufax had ever started in organized baseball.

Koufax may have started some games in a sandlot baseball league in the early 1950s. There are reports that he pitched a bit for the Parkviews of the Coney Island Sports League. There are no records of those games that this writer can find.

That's quite a bit of difference in experience between the 2 Dodgers' rookie pitchers - Roebuck and Koufax.

The Nightcap

The 1st batter Koufax faced, in his first major league start, was the Pirates' rookie Roberto Clemente. He walked him. But he quickly got Clemente off the basepaths when he struck out the 2nd batter, Dick Cole, swinging, and Dodgers' catcher Rube Walker threw a pick off throw to Gil Hodges at 1st base. Hodges put the tag on Clemente for an unusual double play.

However, nothing seems "usual" when we're talking about Sandy Koufax.

Koufax proceeded to walk the next 2 Pirates. But he got out of the inning when he got Dale Long to line out to Jim Gilliam in right field.

Gilliam then drove home Don Zimmer in the top of the 2nd to give Koufax a 1 - 0 lead.

In the bottom of the 2nd, Koufax got the leadoff batter to line out to 3rd base. Then he walked 2 and struck out 2, to get out of the inning and maintain his 1-0 lead.

In the 3rd inning both teams went down in order.

Koufax had now pitched 3 shutout innings and still led the game 1 - 0.

The 4th was another easy inning for Koufax as he allowed just 1 walk.

That made it 4 shutout innings for Koufax.

In the 5th, Koufax got the leadoff batter, Vern Law, on a strikeout. Then he gave up what Jack Lang in the Staten Island Advance referred to as ***"scratch singles*** (that didn't leave the infield)***"*** to Clemente and Cole. The next batter hit a grounder that moved the runners to 2nd and 3rd. With 2 outs and 2 runners in scoring position, Koufax walked Frank Thomas to load the bases.

Next up was Dale Long. Koufax walked him as well. And that brought in the 1st run against Koufax. It also tied the game at 1.

Dodgers' manager Walt Alston decided it was time to take out Sandy. He turned to his trusted rookie Roebuck. Roebuck struck out the next batter to end the threat. He then kept the Pirates in check in the 6th and 7th innings. But in the bottom of the 8th, Roebuck gave up 3 runs and the Dodgers lost the game 4 - 1.

Koufax had looked promising but also wild in his 1st start. Yes, he had only been charged with 1 run and had only yielded 3 hits, all singles, but he had also issued 8 walks in just 4 and 2/3 innings.

But this performance was strong enough that Newsday wrote, ***"KOUFAX GLITTERS,"*** in the headline for the game. In the article, they added, ***"his stuff was impressive... the kid gave up only three hits. Two were infield blows off the gloves of Pee Wee Reese and Don Hoak. The other was a roller through short after Pee Wee Reese had stepped toward second."***

The portion of the article on Koufax concluded that Sandy, ***"was untouchable."***

Newsday also indicated that the reason Alston removed him in the 5th was because Koufax had developed, ***"a kink in his back."***

The New York Daily News's Dick Young however, made it clear that this was a yanking of the starter by Alston. Young noted that Koufax had already thrown 106 pitches in just half a game, and in addition to walking 8 batters, he had gone to a 3 and 2 count on almost everyone he faced.

But Young was not all negative about the bonus baby. He put forth his prescient assessment of Sandy Koufax, ***"Make no mistake about Sandy; he has talent. If nothing happens to his arm, he could become a tremendous winner for Brooklyn. He fires bullets. He has a big, straight-down motion; whipping the ball from behind his left ear. He figures to be wild for now, and he can win in spite of it."***

NOTE from the Present Time

I have come back to the present time to inform you that Dick Young was regarded as one of the great sportswriters of his time. The above evaluation of Koufax's prospects, based on such a limited opportunity to observe him in action, demonstrates why Dick Young is so revered.

Now back to 1955 for one more note.

Additional Dodgers' Notes

Duke Snider is outplaying his rival centerfielders in the New York area this summer by a wide margin.

The Duke leads the majors in home runs with 28.

He also leads the majors in RBIs with 87 in just 80 Dodgers' games. Second most in the majors is just 68 RBIs by Jackie Jensen of the Red Sox.

And Snider is batting .323, which is 4th in the National League and 7th in the majors.

Here's the comparison of the three great New York centerfielders across the 3 major offensive categories through the games of July 6, 1955:

Home Runs

28 Snider

25 Mays

18 Mantle

Runs Batted In

87 Snider

61 Mays

57 Mantle

Batting Average

.323 Snider

.303 Mantle

.296 Mays

The Sports Time Traveler will continue following the 1955 Brooklyn Dodgers day-by-day and filing reports when there is something so fascinating I just have to share it.

Chapter Nine

Newking the National League

Don Newcombe is having the most incredible season

EBBETS FIELD - July 16, 1955

The Sports Time Traveler is continuing to follow the 1955 Dodgers day-by-day.

Yesterday the Dodgers played a mid-week day game at Ebbets Field that sadly only attracted 7,929 fans. This is quite astonishing. The Dodgers are having an unbelievable season. They came into the game with a 58 - 27 record and a 10.5 game lead in the National League over the Milwaukee Braves.

What's more, Don Newcombe was the scheduled pitcher. Newk is having a phenomenal year. He entered the game with a gaudy 14 - 1 record.

How was it that the Dodgers couldn't attract fans to watch this show?

What a Show it Was

Brooklyn fans who had better things to do yesterday missed out on something really special. The Cardinals were in town, and that meant they could have seen Stan "The Man" Musial play.

34-year-old Stan Musial is having yet another solid season. He's 2nd in the NL in RBIs with 67, although he's not even in sniffing distance of the leader, Dodgers' centerfielder Duke Snider who already has 90.

But Stan has something Duke doesn't - the afterglow of hitting the most dramatic home run in All-Star game history. Stan did that this past Tuesday in Milwaukee when he led off the 12th inning with a walk off home run.

NOTE from The Sports Time Traveler

You can watch that home run on YouTube by typing into the search bar, "1955 Major League Baseball All Star Game won by Stan Musial Homer."

Now back to 1955.

Newk faces Stan

In yesterday's game, Don Newcombe got Musial to strike out swinging to finish off a 1-2-3 side in the top of the 1st.

In the bottom of the 2nd, Newk singled and scored the Dodgers' first run.

Newk faced Musial again in the top of the 4th. He got him to hit a grounder to retire the side again.

Newk had pitched to the minimum number of batters through 4 innings.

In the bottom of the inning, Newk had his 2nd at bat and he hit a double.

So now Musial was 0 for 2 and Newk was 2 for 2.

Dodgers 4 Cardinals 0 - End of 4 innings

Musial finally managed a single off Newk in the 6th. But Newk reached based for a 3rd time in the game in the bottom of the inning on an error.

In the top of the 8th, Newk got Stan to ground out again.

While in the bottom of the 8th Newk blasted a home run to deep right field.

Newk's bomb put the Dodgers up 6 - 3. And it started a 6-run rally that sealed the game as the Dodgers' led 12 - 3 after 8 innings.

A Home Run Record for Newk

This was Don Newcombe's 6th home run of the season. That tied him for most home runs in one season by a National League pitcher, and it's only the middle of July!

Newk's home run prowess is so great that he now leads the majors in lowest at bat to home run ratio.

Newk now has 6 home runs in 70 at bats for an at bats to home run ratio of 11.7.

Ted Kluszewski, who leads the majors in home runs with 29, has had 361 at bats for an at bats to home run ratio of 12.5.

I find this statistic so unbelievable that I just have to dwell on this for another moment. A pitcher, who is on his way to holding a 15 - 1 record, almost unprecedented in baseball history, is also the most efficient home run hitter in baseball at the same time.

Images of Babe Ruth

This got me thinking did Babe Ruth ever have a season like this?

NO!

In none of the seasons in which Ruth started 20+ games as a pitcher did he ever hit more than 4 home runs.

In 1919, when he started 15 games and won 9, he hit 29 home runs. And his at bats to home run ratio that year was just 14.9.

Ruth never had a season like Newk is having here in 1955.

It Gets Better

If that wasn't enough to draw more fans to Ebbets Field, here's one more stat that really puts the icing on the cake.

In that 6 run 8th inning yesterday, Newk came up a 2nd time, and slashed a single to drive in the Dodgers' 12th run.

With that single, Newk not only had his 2nd hit of the inning. He not only had his 3rd RBI of the game. He not only had reached base for the 5th time in 5 plate appearances. But Don Newcombe had raised his batting average to .406!

That's right. Don Newcombe, the best starting pitcher in baseball here in 1955, who has just raised his record to 15 - 1, is also batting .406!

Of course, Newk doesn't qualify for the batting title. At this point in the season, the official league leading hitter is Newk's battery mate, Roy Campanella who has well more than the minimum 200 at bats. Campy went 3 for 4 in the game and that raised his average to .345. Campy wasn't quite as good as Newk in the game who was officially 4 for 5 (the time he reached base on error technically counted as an out).

And by the way, Newk held the great Stan Musial to just 1 for 4 batting in the game.

Will Brooklyn Please Support the Dodgers?

With Don Newcombe, Roy Campanella, and Duke Snider all having career years it's no wonder Brooklyn is dominating the National League.

Now, someone has to get the word out in Brooklyn that fans need to actually come out and watch the games or the Dodgers just might have to consider re-locating somewhere else.

The Sports Time Traveler will continue following the 1955 Dodgers wherever they play.

Chapter Ten

The Brooklyn Birthday Bash

The Little Colonel's birthday is celebrated at Ebbets Field like no one else's before

EBBETS FIELD - Saturday July 23, 1955

The Sports Time Traveler has been following the 1955 Dodgers, and it seems that nearly every day, there is something unexpected I find, on this virtual journey back in time.

Last night was no exception.

After drawing just 6,516 fans to Thursday afternoon's victory over the Cubs, the Dodgers put a tiny ad in the New York Times on Friday morning to promote their Friday night and Saturday games against the 2nd place Braves.

What wasn't mentioned in the ad was that the Friday night game was going to feature a big birthday bash for the Dodgers' captain, shortstop Pee Wee Reese.

But the fans knew about the planned birthday celebration from newspaper articles and other sources, and as a result, the Dodgers drew their largest crowd of the season, 33,003 fans for Friday night's festivities.

Pee Wee Reese turned 37 yesterday. On Thursday, he played his 1,800th game for the Dodgers, going back to April 24, 1940, when Reese replaced Leo Durocher as the Dodgers' starting shortstop. Now, 15 years later, only the legendary Zack Wheat has appeared in more games in franchise history.

Jack Lang, writing in the Staten Island Advance, described the birthday celebration that took an entire hour prior to the start of the game, ***"It was a night to remember, for the fans as much as for Reese."***

Dick Young in the New York Daily News called it, ***"The most lavish birthday party in Brooklyn history."***

Pee Wee received about 50 gifts in the pre-game ceremony. Some of the gifts were:

- portable typewriter
- freezer filled with 200 pounds of beef, shrimp and lobster rolls
- TV
- movie camera and sound projector
- still camera with a year's supply of film and flash bulbs
- tape recorder
- gift certificates for clothing
- 2 sets of golf clubs
- 100 pounds of coffee
- 1,000 tea bags
- hunting coat
- fishing tackle
- $100 dollars' worth of Arthur Murray dance lessons
- lifetime invitation to Grossinger's (a Catskill mountains resort)
- 2 sets of tires

Oh, and there were also gifts for Reese's wife and daughter, as noted by Dick Young, ***"For Mrs. Reese there was a vacuum cleaner, and for daughter Barbara, a set of encyclopedia, a bicycle, and numerous toys and games."***

And there was more!

Pee Wee received gifts of cash from the fans as reported by Dick Young, ***"Cash contributions from the fans were presented to Pee Wee in the form of three $1,000 U.S. Savings Bonds. This denomination, in case you haven't bought one lately, bears the picture of Abraham Lincoln."***

And that still was not all. No, that was not all!

The biggest gift of the day was delivered in the most dramatic fashion.

Seven new cars rolled onto the field.

The cars ranged from economy to luxury. Reese would receive one of them.

Pee Wee's 11 year old daughter Barbara was given the task of determining which set of wheels her father would receive in game show like format.

Barbara had to pick 1 key out of a fish bowl and then see which car door it opened.

Jack Lang described the fans' reaction in Ebbets as the crowd saw which car the key did not and ultimately did unlock:

But in spite of all the presents for Pee Wee, the New York Times wrote, ***"The kind words outnumbered the gifts.***

More than a dozen people were brought up to speak, including baseball commissioner Ford Frick and the scout that discovered Pee Wee - Ted McGrew.

There were also telegrams sent by famous dignitaries that were read to the crowd. These included messages from:

- Vice President Nixon

- General Douglas MacArthur

- Senator Alben Barkley of Reese's home state of Kentucky

- Governor of Kentucky, Lawrence Wetherby

- Mayor of Louisville, Andrew Broadus.

And then Pee Wee himself spoke to the fans in Ebbets Field, ***"When I came to Brooklyn in 1940, I was a scared kid. I'm twice as scared right now."***

But even that wasn't the highlight of the ceremonies. That honor went to Reese's mother. She was brought out to home plate in a total surprise to Pee Wee. It seems that Pee Wee had been told that his mother could not make it to Brooklyn for the birthday party.

A Game is Played!

Oh, and yes, after an hour of festivities, the game actually began and when it did the Milwaukee Braves helped contribute to the birthday atmosphere.

After rookie Roger Craig, pitching in just his 2nd major league game, set down the Braves in order in the top of the 1st, the Dodgers' Don Hoak led off with a single and that brought up the 37 year old birthday boy to the plate. Reese is having a solid season batting . 283 coming into the game.

Pee Wee promptly slashed a double to right field that drove in Hoak and the Dodgers took a 1 - 0 lead.

In the top of the 2nd, Craig must have felt good after he struck out Hank Aaron. But then he gave up a homer to Joe Adcock that tied the game.

The Dodgers went right back in the lead in the bottom of the 2nd when Carl Furillo singled home Junior Gilliam.

But Craig lost the lead again when he gave up a leadoff homer in the 3rd to Del Crandall.

And yet again, the Dodgers went back up 3 - 2 when Gil Hodges smashed a homer in the 4th.

More Festivities

As if the game had not been delayed enough in Pee Wee's honor, at the end of the 5th inning a break was taken for birthday cake!

The New York Times reported, ***"Two giant birthday cakes were wheeled out to home plate. At a signal from Happy Felton over the microphone, all lights were turned out and every fan in the stands lit either a match or a cigarette lighter and sang Happy Birthday."***

NOTE from The Sports Time Traveler

Happy Felton was an entertainer who hosted a pre-game TV show on WOR channel 9 in the New York area called, "Happy Felton's Knothole Gang." The show took place about half an hour before each game at Ebbets Field and was filmed from the right field bullpen and included three little league players who had been selected to be on the show for a particular game based on their performance in their leagues.

Back to Baseball

In the top of the 6th, Craig gave up his 3rd homer, this one to Hank Aaron. The game was tied once again at 3.

But in the bottom of the 6th, Pee Wee led off with his 2nd double of the game. And he scored moments later on a Gil Hodges sacrifice fly. When Pee Wee crossed home plate, the Dodgers were back in front 4 - 3.

But one more time, Roger Craig gave up a home run, the 4th he allowed in the game, and the 2nd one to Del Crandall, and the game was knotted up at 4 - 4.

A Birthday Present from the Braves

An inning later it was the Milwaukee Braves' turn to deliver a present to Reese.

In the bottom of the 7th, with one out and runners on 2nd and 3rd, Pee Wee Reese made his 4th plate appearance. Newsday described what happened as Pee Wee faced the Braves' Gene Conley, ***"He made an unintentional half-swing at one of Gene Conley's pitches and rolled a miserable dribbler toward first as the 33,003 fans moaned. But Adcock, in the spirit of the occasion, politely fumbled the ball and Carl Furillo strode over the plate."***

Reese had put the Dodgers back in front 5 - 4.

In the top of the 8th, Ed Roebuck came in to pitch after Roger Craig had been lifted for a pinch hitter in the 7th. With 2 outs and Hank Aaron on 2nd base, Chuck Tanner hit a grounder to the left side of the infield. Newsday wrote that Pee Wee, ***"made the decisive play of the eighth inning"*** as he got to the ball and threw Tanner out at 1st base.

The Dodgers had retained their slim 5 - 4 lead.

The contest was finally put to rest when Carl Furillo blasted a 3-run homer in the bottom of the 8th, and the Dodgers went on to win it 8 - 4.

In fitting fashion, Reese had a fantastic game on his birthday, with 2 doubles, an RBI and what turned out to be the winning run produced on the gift error by Adcock on Reese's ground ball in the 7th.

And that was not all!

The Times reported that, ***"At 11:05pm it was announced to the crowd that Walter O'Malley*** (the Dodgers' owner) ***had just received a cablegram from the President of the United States extending his best wishes to Pee Wee Reese."***

With the victory, the Dodgers are now 65 - 29 and have a 14.5 game lead in the National League over the 2nd place Milwaukee Braves.

This afternoon is Ladies Day at Ebbets Field with game time at 2pm. The Sports Time Traveler is eagerly awaiting tomorrow's newspapers to find out the results.

Chapter Eleven

The Relief Hitter

ST. LOUIS - July 30, 1955

The Sports Time Traveler is following the 1955 Dodgers day-by-day, and it's been one thrill after another this month, much more than I ever expected when I embarked on this virtual time travel journey back in March.

Yesterday, the Boys of Summer were on the road at Busch Stadium in St. Louis to face Stan Musial and the Cardinals. The Dodgers are the best hitting team in baseball this year, and the Cardinals sent a rookie, Larry Jackson, to the mound.

Jackson showed promise in the minors, he was 12 - 6 in AAA last year in 1954. And back in 1952, playing for Fresno in the California League, he had one of the greatest seasons in minor league history, posting a record of 28 - 4. But now in the big leagues, he's struggling. He came into the game with a 5 - 7 record and a 4.42 ERA. And in his last start, he gave up 6 runs in 2 and 2/3 innings, against the Phillies.

Yet Jackson started the game like he was California Dreaming. In the top of the 1st, he got Don Hoak to pop up. Then he gave up singles to Pee Wee Reese and Duke Snider. Already Jackson was in a jam with the National League's leading hitter and 2-time MVP Roy Campanella coming up. But Jackson got Campy to hit a double play ball to 2nd baseman Red Schoendienst, and that put a "0" up on the scoreboard for the Dodgers.

In the 2nd, Jackson got the Dodgers in order as Gil Hodges flew out. Jim Gilliam grounded out and Carl Furillo struck out swinging.

In the 3rd, Jackson got Pee Wee Reese to hit into a side-ending double play.

In the 4th, inning Jackson faced the biggest Brooklyn batters - Snider, Campanella and Hodges. Snider walked, but Campy hit into a double play and Hodges grounded out to short. What a thrill that must have been for the rookie Jackson to get through the Dodgers' power hitters.

The 5th was another 1-2-3 inning for Jackson.

In the 6th Jackson faced his biggest threat yet. With 2 outs and Reese on 2nd and Snider on 1st, Walt Alston called for a double steal, and it worked. Now with 2 Dodgers in scoring position, Campy came up. Jackson got him to hit a grounder to short, and the rookie had now registered 6 shutout innings against the dangerous Dodger bats.

Meanwhile the Cardinals had put up 3 runs on Dodgers' starter Karl Spooner, one of them on an RBI single by Stan "The Man" Musial.

Spooner was an interesting young pitcher for the Dodgers. He had come up right near the end of the 1954 season, and in his only 2 games, he threw a 3-hit shutout on September 22nd against the eventual World Series champion Giants, and a 4-hit shutout on September 26th. It looked like the Dodgers might have a new star pitcher.

But in his first start in 1955, he couldn't get out of the 3rd inning against the Reds. And he came into yesterday's game with a 2 - 4 record and a 4.88 ERA.

Spooner gave up 3 runs on 5 hits through the first 6 innings, and the Cardinals led the game 3 - 0 after 6.

Now, in the top of the 7th, the Dodgers had to make something happen if they were going to get back in this game. Gil Hodges led off with a single against Larry Jackson. But Jackson got Gilliam and Furillo to fly out.

Don Zimmer kept the inning alive with a single. Now the pitcher Karl Spooner was due up. Walt Alston had no choice but to lift Spooner for a pinch hitter even though there were 2 outs.

Fortunately for Alston he has a player on his bench who came into the game with the National League's best batting average at .388, although he doesn't officially qualify since he has under 100 at bats. The player is also Alston's ace pitcher - Don Newcombe.

Newk stepped in against Larry Jackson. Dick Young of the New York Daily News wrote about the scene, ***"If you don't think Don has become something of a terror with that bat, you should have seen the commotion his presence at the plate created. First, Schoendienst and back stop Burbrink came to the mound to counsel Jackson. The Bird pitcher threw two cautious balls to Newk - and then manager Harry Walker came running out to advise Jax. Either the advice was poor or Jackson failed to heed it."***

Newk blasted Jackson's next pitch 380 feet to deep left center.

John Craig reported in the Newark Star Ledger, ***"Don Newcombe pinch hit and rapped one of Jackson's serves to deep left center and, for a few moments, it appeared that the ball was heading into the stands. It faded and a fan reached out of the bleachers and touched it. The hit was ruled a ground rule double and Zimmer, who had scored from first, had to go back to third.***

Gil Hodges scored. Newk had a double and possibly had been robbed of a game-tying 3-run homer. And the Dodgers were finally on the board.

The next batter was leadoff hitter Don Hoak. On the first pitch, Hoak made things right for Dodgers' fans. He blasted a 3-run homer, scoring Zimmer from 3rd and Newcombe from 2nd.

Suddenly, Brooklyn was ahead 4 - 3.

And Larry Jackson, who had pitched 6 superb innings, had thrown 2 bad pitches in a row that resulted in 4 runs, all scoring with 2 outs. Jackson was knocked out of the game.

Brooklyn went on to win the game 5 - 4 with Clem Labine shutting down the Cardinals in the last 2 innings.

The win officially went to relief pitcher Clem Labine, but his fellow pitcher Don Newcombe, in a "relief hitting" role, supplied the big hit that changed the course of the game for the Dodgers.

Newk, who sports a 17 - 1 record as a starter, one of the greatest beginnings to any major league season for a pitcher, is having a dream year so far. He is now batting .395 with 8 doubles, 6 homers and 19 RBIs in just 85 at bats.

If you extrapolate those stats over a 600 at bat season, Newk would be on pace for 40+ home runs and 100+ RBIs, while batting close to .400.

Should the Dodgers be considering Newk as an everyday player a la Babe Ruth in 1920? It's time to start the discussion.

The win was the 69th of the season for the Dodgers against just 32 losses. They remain 12.5 games in front of the Braves on top of the National League.

And guess who is coming to the mound today in St. Louis? Don Newcombe. The Sports Time Traveler can't wait!

The Sports Time Traveler will continue following the 1955 Dodgers daily.

Chapter Twelve

Baseball's Most Devastating Duo

ST. LOUIS - August 1, 1955

The Sports Time Traveler was in St. Louis for a Sunday afternoon sizzler here in 1955 yesterday. The temperatures reached about 100 degrees as the Dodgers played the final game of a 3 game set against the Cardinals.

I was very excited for this game because Don Newcombe was starting for Brooklyn. Newcombe came into the game with a record of 17 - 1.

And Newcombe started the game by striking out the Cards' shortstop Bob Stephenson on his way to a 1-2-3 inning.

In the 2nd inning, the Dodgers put 2 runs on the board before Don Newcombe came to the plate for the first time with just 1 out. In addition to his otherworldly 17 - 1 record, Newcombe also sports the best batting average in major league baseball for anyone with more than 80 at bats. He's hitting .395. And Newk has been particularly harsh on Cardinals' pitchers this season. Against the Cards, he's hitting .647 (11 for 17).

What took place next you might never find again in the coverage of a major league baseball game. The Cardinals walked the pitcher, Don Newcombe, so they could get to the weaker hitters at the top of the Brooklyn batting order.

The strategy worked for Cardinals' manager Harry Walker as both leadoff man Don Hoak, and #2 batter Pee Wee Reese, stranded Newk on first and the side was retired.

Newk had the short walk from first base to the mound to pitch to the Cardinals in the bottom of the 2nd. His time on the mound was almost as short as his stay was on 1st base. Newk only faced the minimum 3 batters.

Dodgers 2 Cardinals 0 - end of 2 innings

In the top of the 3rd, Newcombe's roommate, catcher Roy Campenella, came to the plate. Campy leads the National League in batting for all players with more than 100 at bats at .331. He whacked one into the left field bleachers. It was his 23rd homer of the year and the 200th of his career. He is now the 3rd all-time leading HR hitter among catchers, trailing only Gabby Hartnett (236) and Bill Dickey (202).

In the bottom of the 3rd, Newk had another 1-2-3 inning. But he did it with the help of the Duke, centerfielder Duke Snider.

Snider is the often overlooked "3rd centerfielder" in New York City. In a town that has the reigning MVP and 1954 World Series hero Willie Mays playing centerfield for the Giants, and the already legendary Mickey Mantle, who has 3 World Series titles under his belt with the Yankees, it's easy to relegate Duke Snider to the status of 3rd best centerfielder in New York.

But this year things are different. Duke is having a year almost as good as Don Newcombe. The Duke presently leads the majors in home runs with 35 and RBIs with 104. And he's 3rd in the National League in batting average just .007 behind his teammate Roy Campanella.

Duke is also a great fielding centerfielder, and yesterday he gave a fine example.

With 2 outs in the bottom of the 3rd, Cardinals' pitcher Floyd Wooldridge faced Newcombe. Wooldridge drilled a line drive into centerfield.

Here's what Harry Mitauer wrote in the St. Louis Globe-Democrat about this play:

"Duke Snider, the Dodgers center fielder, turned in a sparkling catch to take a hit away from Floyd Woolridge in the third inning. Running at great speed, he made a diving catch that brought the fans up cheering."

Oh, how I would love to have seen video of that catch. Perhaps it would have made New Yorkers appreciate the Duke much more.

It's also quite astonishing that fans in St. Louis would stand up and cheer a catch by an opposing center fielder. It had to be an astonishing play.

With the side retired, through 3 innings, Don Newcombe had faced the minimum number of Cardinals.

Dodgers 3 Cardinals 0 - end of 3 innings

In the bottom of the 4th, with the score still 3 - 0 Dodgers, Newcombe got the leadoff batter out. Next up was 2nd baseman Red Schoendienst. Red crushed a ball that landed on top of the roof in right field to make it 3 - 1.

The next batter was Stan "The Man" Musial. Musial had faced Newcombe 60 times prior to this at bat and had never hit a home run. He broke the streak in spectacular style as he hit one completely over the roof in right and out of the ballpark.

Musial's blast landed on Grand Avenue, according to Harry Mitauer in the St. Louis Globe-Democrat.

Suddenly, Newk looked like he was in trouble. The Cardinals had made it a ballgame with the score now 3 - 2 Dodgers. But more than that, the momentum had shifted to the home team Cardinals, and Dodgers' manager Walt Alston had to be wondering what was up with Newk.

But there was no panic from the Boys of Summer. Newk went right back to work and got the clean-up batter, Wally Moon, for a swing and a miss 3rd strike. A few moments later, Newk was out of the inning with his lead intact when he got Joe Frazier (no, not the boxer) on a flyball to the Duke in centerfield.

Dodgers 3 Cardinals 2 - end of 4 innings

The rest of the game turned into a laugher for the Dodgers. They scored 3 runs in the 5th, another in the 6th, and 4 more in the 8th.

Meanwhile Newk was masterful on the mound, allowing just one single the rest of the way.

Brooklyn won the game 11 - 2.

3 of the 11 runs were driven in by Campanella, who went 4 for 5 on the day to raise his league leading batting average to .339.

And with the complete game 5-hitter, Don Newcombe raised his record to an unbelievable 18 - 1.

Only 1 pitcher in major league history has had a better start to a season than Don Newcombe in 1955. Rube Marquard, of the New York Giants, started the 1912 season at 19 - 0. Newcombe is just a single game behind the Rube.

Newk and Campy, the pitcher and the catcher, and roommates on the road, are likely the most devastating duo in baseball here in 1955.

But while Newk's record as a pitcher soared to near record heights yesterday, at the plate, the Cardinals finally conquered Newk. After walking in the 1st inning, he grounded into a double play in the 4th, grounded out again leading off both the 6th and the 8th innings, and, in the 9th inning, Newcombe came up one more time, and he didn't waste any energy, looking at 3 pitches for a quick strikeout.

With an 0 for 4 game, Newk's batting average dropped to .376.

The Pennant Race

It is now August 1st, the traditional day on which it said the pennant races start.

The Dodgers are sitting high on top of the National League with a record 71 - 32.

Here are the standings as of this morning:

71 – 32 Brooklyn Dodgers

57 – 45 Milwaukee Braves

54 – 50 New York Giants

53 – 54 Philadelphia Phillies

50 – 56 Chicago Cubs

45 – 54 St. Louis Cardinals

46 – 56 Cincinnati Reds

38 – 67 Pittsburgh Pirates

The Dodgers lead by 13.5 games, but they know they can't get complacent or start thinking it's wrapped up. The Boys of Summer all remember that just 4 years ago, on August 11, 1951, they led the Giants by 13 games... and lost the pennant.

The Sports Time Traveler is going to continue to follow the 1955 Dodgers daily and report back to you when there is again a story so compelling I just have to share it.

Chapter Thirteen

... And The Duke

Here in 1955, Duke Snider is challenging Babe Ruth's record whether he wants to or not

WRIGLEY FIELD - August 7, 1955

The Sports Time Traveler has been back in time virtually, following the 1955 Dodgers day-by-day since spring training. I never expected that on this day, August 7, 1955, the newspapers across the country would be talking about Babe Ruth. After all the Babe had retired 20 years ago, and had been sadly gone since 1948.

Why was the Babe in the news?

Yesterday afternoon, the Dodgers and Cubs game was delayed by 1 hour and 15 minutes due to weather. When there was a break in the rain they began play. Just 11 minutes later the rain came back with a vengeance and the game was called off.

With nothing to do, reporters had lots of time to interview Duke Snider. The Duke, along with the Cubs' young slugger, 24-year-old shortstop, Ernie Banks, and the Reds' burly 1st baseman Ted Kluszewski, are making an assault on Babe Ruth's hallowed number of 60 home runs - the exalted single season record the Sultan of Swat set 28 years ago in 1927.

Here's what the 1955 major league home run list looks like as of this morning (8/7/1955):

38 Duke Snider

37 Ernie Banks

36 Ted Kluszewski

34 Willie Mays

29 Eddie Mathews

28 Wally Post

24 Mickey Mantle

At first glance they appear to have a long way to go to 60. But sportswriters have some historical statistics available to them, even here in 1955, and they know that Babe Ruth did not hit No. 38 until his 115th game of the 1927 season.

Snider has 38 home runs in just 108 games! He's more than a week's worth of games ahead of Ruth.

Banks has 37 home runs in 112 games. That puts Banks ahead of the Bambino's pace too. Ruth didn't hit his 37th home run until his 114th game.

And the Chicago Tribune pointed out this morning that Banks has hit 19 home runs just since July 1st, including 3 in one game on August 4th. That puts Banks on a clear trajectory to catch Ruth.

And Ted Kluszewski also has a case. He has 36 home runs in 109 games. Ruth didn't hit No. 36 until his 110th game.

All 3 of these sluggers are AHEAD of Babe Ruth's 60 HR pace from 1927.

And that was big news today across America.

The New York Times ran an article at the top of page 83 of the Sunday paper with the headline, ***"Dodgers Snider Admits Dilemma."*** Beat writer Roscoe McGowen interviewed Duke. Here's what Roscoe wrote, ***"the possibility of breaking Babe Ruth's 1927 record of sixty homers got into the conversation, with Snider making an unusual statement. 'I hope nobody ever***

breaks Babe's record,' said the Duke. 'Of course, if it does happen, I'd like to be the fellow who does it.'

'But,' he added, 'I really hope it is never broken. Ruth was baseball and all of us today are profiting by what he did. He made the game for the kids and for all of us.'"

The New York Daily News ran an article titled, ***"Snider Hoping Ruth's Mark Stands."*** Dick Young of the Daily News recounted what McGowen wrote and added this, ***"Snider revealed that he and Ted Kluszewski, Cincy's entry in the new Ruth derby, sometimes discuss the record target, and the influence of ballparks on their chances of breaking it.***

'Ted said,' reports Duke, 'that if he faced as much right-handed pitching as I do, he'd have a good shot at the record. I agree with that, but I told him that if I played in his park, and still saw as much righty pitching as we get, I'd probably beat him to it.'"

The two players were referring to the fact that as the only big lefty hitter in the Dodgers' lineup, opposing managers often pitch only righty pitchers against the Dodgers. Just this past week, the Braves skipped lefty Warren Spahn in the rotation against the Dodgers just so he wouldn't have to face all those righty bats.

Snider was also contending that the fence in right-center in Cincinnati actually comes in creating a very short shot for hitting home runs.

Even in North Carolina, the Salisbury Post ran an article with a headline, ***"Snider, Banks Ahead of Babe Ruth's Pace."*** This was an Associated Press piece that opened with this line, ***"Brooklyn's Duke Snider and Ernie Bank of the Chicago Cubs - both pushing ahead of Babe Ruth's home run record for one season - have created new interest in the National League."***

And yesterday in Chicago, for a brief time fans could see both Duke and Ernie. They posed for a picture, each in their batting stance with their bats held high and facing each other, Duke the lefty and Ernie the righty. That classic picture ran in many newspapers across the nation.

Duke Snider is finally getting the national recognition he deserves.

NOTE From The Sports Time Traveler

I interrupt this article with a note from the present time. For the past 40+ years I've always loved hearing the song, "Talkin Baseball," by Terry Cashman. In the chorus of the song is the now iconic phrase, *"Willie, Mickey and the Duke."*

Cashman was referring to the 3 great centerfielders on the 3 New York teams of the mid-1950s. It was a golden era in New York baseball, and each team was, in a way, defined by their great centerfielders.

By 1955, 24-year-old Willie Mays was already a legend. He was the "Say Hey Kid." He had won the 1954 NL MVP, and made "The Catch" in game 1 of the 1954 World Series. "The Catch," generally regarded as the greatest catch in history, inspired the Giants to sweep the 111 win Cleveland Indians for the title - one of the most shocking World Series upsets ever.

By 1955, 23-year-old Mickey Mantle already had won 3 World Series titles with the Yankees, amply taking over centerfield from Joe DiMaggio, and continuing the dynasty. He had also hit the famous "tape measure shot," in 1953, one of the longest home runs ever recorded. Mickey was the clear successor to the Bambino and Joltin' Joe, an iconic figure who would keep the Yankees as the perpetual team to beat for another decade.

Duke Snider was their equal. In fact, on paper, in 1955, he was superior. Snider was 29 in 1955. He was coming off 6 straight sensational seasons from 1949 - 1954 and was in the midst of a 7th in 1955. On August 7, 1955, Snider led the majors in HRs, RBIs, and was among the leaders in batting average. He was a true triple crown threat.

But Snider had no World Series title. The Brooklyn Dodgers had never won a World Series in their franchise history going into 1955. And so the Duke was by default the 3rd man of the trio in stature. It's Willie, Mickey, and The Duke is a distant 3rd in the pantheon of New York baseball.

Now back to 1955.

As mentioned before, yesterday's game was rained out, but the day prior, on August 5th, in the first game of the series, the Dodgers and Cubs played one of the most entertaining games I've ever read about.

First of all, how crazy is this. Another day earlier, on August 4th, both the Dodgers and the Cubs won games by a score of 11 - 10. I wonder how often that has ever happened.

And both teams won in late inning come from behind rallies after being ahead early in the game.

In the Cubs case, they blew a 9 - 2 lead and found themselves down 10 - 9 in the 8th. It took 3 home runs from Ernie Banks, the last of which turned out to be the game winner, to seal the victory over the Pirates.

As a result, Ernie Banks came into the August 5th game tied with Duke Snider for the major league lead at 36.

The Duke quickly broke the tie in the top of the 1st inning when he slammed his 37th. It was a tremendous shot. Roscoe McGowen of the New York Times wrote, "(the) ***smash nearly reached the back barrier of the right-centerfield bleachers."***

In the bottom of the 1st, Banks evened the score, again depositing a Johnny Podres pitch deep into the left-centerfield seats for his No. 37, and his 4th home run in his last 6 at bats.

In the top of the 5th, Duke Snider swung at the first pitch from Warren Hacker and, ***"The Duke sent it screeching into the street behind the right field for No. 38,"*** as described by Irving Vaughan in the Chicago Tribune.

As a Dodgers fan you have to love it when the other cities' beat writers refer to Snider as "The Duke."

Snider had pulled Brooklyn within a run at 7 - 6 in this high scoring affair.

The Cubs had a 10 - 8 lead going into the 9th inning. The Dodgers were down to their last at bats, but they had Duke Snider leading off. Russ McGowen of the New York Times wrote, "***The Duke opened the ninth with a tremendous***

drive." But the wind, which had shifted in the middle of the game, held the ball in the park and it was caught by Eddie Miksis up against the right field wall."

Duke had come oh so close to a 3 homer game, just like Banks had done the day before.

After Snider made the 1st out, the Dodgers managed to put 2 runners on base and a few minutes later Carl Furillo hit a drive way back in deep centerfield. But the wind held this one up as well and it was caught to end the game. The Cubs won 10 - 8.

Dodgers' coach Billy Herman told Jack Lang in the Staten Island Advance after the game, ***"There's no park in baseball where the wind makes such a difference."***

Even though the Dodgers (74 - 34) lost the game, they retained a whopping 15.5 game lead over the Braves who also lost to the last place Pirates.

And while the Dodgers - Cubs game was rained out yesterday, the 2nd place Braves were shutout at home by Bob Friend of the Pittsburgh Pirates. That means the Dodgers now have a 16 game lead on the National League with 46 games left to play.

If the Dodgers play just .500 ball the rest of the way, they would finish 97 - 57, and the Braves, with a record of 58 - 50, would need to post a 40 - 6 record the rest of the way to beat them.

FINAL NOTE From the Sports Time Traveler

In case you'd like to hear Talkin' Baseball and that famous line, *"Willie, Mickey and the Duke,"* you can listen to it on YouTube by searching for "Willie, Mickey and the Duke (Talkin' Baseball)."

The Sports Time Traveler will continue following the 1955 Brooklyn Dodgers and the race to top Babe Ruth's 60 HR record.

Chapter Fourteen

OH! MY! GOSH! 19-Year-Old Koufax

EBBETS FIELD - August 28, 1955

By August 25th, 3 days ago, even the most panicky people had to admit that it looked like the Dodgers had the pennant race wrapped up. Although dem Bums had recently had a stretch of 9 losses in 13 games, they had won their last 2 and so they woke up on 25th of August with their lead at a comfortable 12.5 games with 32 left to play. Joseph Sheehan of the New York Times opened his August 25th article on the Dodgers 9 – 5 victory over the Cubs the prior afternoon with this, ***"The Dodgers doused the feint glimmers of hope that had started to flicker in their distant National League pursuers."***

If the Brooks simply played a little over .500 ball and limped home 17 – 15 in those final 32 contests, the Braves would have to win out. That is the Braves would have to go on an all-time baseball record 29 – 0 winning streak just to win the pennant by a single game.

So perhaps Walter Alston felt it was time to experiment, time to get another look at some of his bench players.

Frank Kellert, who had just 3 pinch-hit appearances in over a month's time was in the starting lineup on August 23rd and 24th and responded going 4 for 8 with

2 homers. That earned him a start in both ends of the doubleheader on August 25th.

And Sandy Koufax got in the first game of the doubleheader on August 25th. It was the 1st time in a month he saw any action. The bonus baby had not thrown a pitch since July 24th. And Koufax had only appeared in 5 games all season, for a total of just 10 and 2/3 innings. In those 5 games, he had given up just 6 hits and 3 earned runs, so he had an ERA of just 2.53 and Hits Per 9 Innings of just 5.06 coming into the August 25th contest.

With numbers like that, you'd think the kid would have been seeing more action.

Yet, Alston has been so flummoxed by Koufax's wildness, his 12 walks in those 10 and 2/3 innings, including 8 in 4 innings in his sole start back in June, that he couldn't see fit to give more time on the mound to this boy, with no prior professional baseball experience.

The only reason Koufax is even wearing a Dodgers' uniform is that the team saw enough future potential in him to grant him an enormous $14,000 signing bonus before the season ($20,000 including his salary of $6,000). And the rules of baseball here in 1955 state that if you give a player a bonus of that amount, you can't park them in the minor leagues. They must remain on the big league roster all season.

Now Koufax was called in for mop up duty in the top of the 9th, in the 1st game of a twilight doubleheader that had gotten out of hand against the Cincinnati Reds. The Dodgers were down 8 – 3. Rookie Ed Roebuck had just come in to pitch the 9th and had been rocked by the Reds. Roebuck who had looked so sharp earlier in the season, sporting a stellar 1.89 ERA near the end of June, was now in the midst of his 5th straight failure. On this night, he couldn't get a single hitter out, giving up 4 consecutive singles. And that's when Walter Alston made the call for Koufax.

As Sandy took the mound in Ebbets Field, the Reds had no outs and big Ted Kluszewski standing on 3rd base and Wally Post on 1st base and Gus Bell at the plate wielding a bat. Bell came into this game batting .306 with 23 homers and 80 RBIs.

On Sandy's 1st pitch to Gus, he got him to swing and miss.

On Sandy's 2nd pitch to Gus, he got him to swing and miss.

On Sandy's 3rd pitch to Gus, he struck him out, on a swing and a miss.

Now with 1 man down, and Kluszewski still standing 90 feet from home, and Post still posing a menacing figure at 1st base, Matt Batts came to bat. Batts had been batting .300 for the past month.

On Sandy's 1st pitch to Matt, he got him to swing and miss.

On Sandy's 2nd pitch to Matt, he got him to swing and miss.

On Sandy's 3rd pitch to Matt, he struck him out, on a swing and a miss.

6 pitches. 6 swinging strikes!

Now with 2 men down and the same 2 men on, up came 3rd baseman Rocky Bridges. Rocky is in the middle of his best season in his career so far, hitting .315 coming into this game.

On Sandy's 1st pitch to Rocky, he got him to swing and miss.

On Sandy's 2nd pitch to Rocky, he got him to swing and miss.

On Sandy's 3rd pitch to Rocky, he got him to hit a fly ball to Frank Kellert at 1st base.

The side was retired. No runs, no hits off Koufax.

Dick Young, writing in the August 26th New York Daily News, penned this, ***"some 17,000 fans at Ebbets Field were cheering wildly. They were cheering, of all people, Sandy Koufax, who had just come in to fire eight straight swinging strikes, and provide the crowd with the one refreshing interlude of a rather drab Dodger performance."***

Sandy had achieved something for which there are no reported accounts of it ever happening previously - 8 straight swinging strikes!

As all baseball fans know there are 3 basic kinds of strikes:

1 – Called strikes

2 – Foul balls

3 – Swinging strikes

Of the 3 types, the swinging strike is by far the most spectacular. Sure, it's nice to hear an umpire bellow a long, slow, loud called 3rd "steeerike!" But there is nothing like watching your team's pitcher throw to one of the opposing team's top hitters and make them whiff at it.

The swinging strike is the most profound, the most dramatic, the most striking.

And here, a 19-year-old, threw 8 straight swinging strikes against 3 quality hitters!

Koufax had lowered his ERA to just 2.31! And his Hits Per 9 Innings had dropped to 4.63!

One more thing about that little stat I slipped in there about Koufax's Hits Per 9 Innings. Of course, no one in here in 1955 has ever heard of a stat like Hits Per 9 Innings, but at this moment, Koufax had the lowest Hits Per 9 Innings in history. Well, he would be #1 in this category if he had the minimum 1,000 innings pitched, instead of just 11.

But it is interesting to note that in all baseball history no one, who qualifies, has ever had less than 6 Hits Per 9 Innings in their career.

And here in 1955, in Koufax's first 11 and 2/3 innings of his career, he was coming in at just 4.63 Hits Per 9 Innings.

After his August 25th performance it should have been quite clear to Walter Alston that the kid can pitch!

NOTE From The Sports Time Traveler

I interrupt this article to come back to the present time and inform you about some further research I did on Koufax's 8 straight swinging strikes. There are sadly no official records kept for consecutive swinging strikes. But there are also no other accounts of anyone ever having more than 8. And there is only one other account of any pitcher getting 8, and it was nearly a half-century after Sandy.

So it's quite possible that in that game, 70 years ago last night, Koufax became the first pitcher in history to throw 8 straight swinging strikes.

Brian Lawrence of the Padres is the only other player ever reported to have done it. On June 12, 2002, Lawrence threw 8 straight swinging strikes. And there is video evidence on YouTube. You can see it by entering the following search terms on YouTube, "Brian Lawrence tosses an immaculate inning." Note that none of the batters Lawrence faced were hitting above .250, and one was hitting below .200.

I also contacted my esteemed colleague Marty Appel about this story.

Marty has spent his career in baseball. For 10 years he worked in the Yankees organization, serving as public relations director during the Reggie Jackson era. He has written 20 books on baseball and he won an EMMY award in 1992 for his work producing Yankee TV broadcasts on WPIX in New York.

Marty was also a friend of New York Daily News sportswriter Dick Young.

Dick Young is the only reporter who made note of Sandy Koufax's 8 straight swinging strikes in newspaper accounts of the game that appeared on August 26, 1955. The only other newspaper in the country that made a similar mention was Newsday. And in the Newsday article, an unnamed reporter indicated Koufax had recorded 8 straight strikes, without distinguishing what kind of strikes they were.

So I asked Marty Appel what he thought about the veracity of Dick Young's report. Marty said, *"when in doubt, trust Young. He was the best."*

Dick Young really was among the best. He is a member of the Baseball Hall of Fame as a writer. And he was a past president of the Baseball Writers' Association of America.

So I have to agree with Marty Appel, a man who knew Dick personally. We should take Dick Young's first-hand account at face value. Sandy Koufax threw 8 straight swinging strikes against quality hitters on the evening of August 25, 1955. Koufax just might be the first pitcher to ever do that. And he was just 19 and pitching in his 6th professional baseball game. Wow!

As the Sports Time Traveler I've had many wonderful experiences taking virtual trips back in time to follow great athletes and sporting events from the distant past. But the most rewarding parts of my hundreds of journeys into the past have been the times I have come across something absolutely unexpected that is of almost unimaginable grandeur.

Finding that Sandy Koufax, at age 19, in just his 6th professional appearance, threw 8 straight swinging strikes, a feat that perhaps had never been done before, and wasn't done again for nearly 50 years, qualifies as one of the incredible sports time travel "discoveries" I have made. And it makes all the time I've spent in the past seem so worthwhile.

Now back to 1955.

Dem Bums and Their Fans are in the Dumps

The 2nd game of the August 25th doubleheader was no better for Brooklyn. The Reds scored twice in the 1st inning off another Dodgers' rookie pitcher Roger Craig.

The Dodgers were still behind 4 - 3 in the 7th inning when Duke Snider came to the plate. Snider was 0 for 7 on the evening, and the fans were booing their star centerfielder according to the AP article that ran nationally. But Snider responded with an RBI single to tie the game.

It's really unconscionable to me that Brooklyn fans could boo the Duke.

But the fans were frustrated that Dodgers' pitchers not named Koufax, couldn't contain the Reds. The Reds forged ahead again in the 9th 6 - 4.

The Dodgers of course had one more chance in the bottom of the 9th. Duke Snider drove in another run to make it 6 - 5 with 2 outs. But Carl Furillo grounded out to end the game.

Snider by the way, now has a major league leading 116 RBIs in just 124 games.

The Braves beat the Giants on that same night, so the Dodgers lead on August 25th was cut down to 11 games. However with just 30 games to go, if the Dodgers could play only .500 ball, the Braves would have to close the season with a 26 - 2 record to win the pennant.

On August 26th, the Dodgers lost again to the Reds by a score of 4 – 2. Sore armed Carl Erskine, who hasn't completed a game since June 10th, gave up all 4 runs in 6 innings of work. And that enabled the Braves to close the gap to 10 games.

The Game of August 27th

Now with a 3 game losing streak and the Dodgers suddenly dwindling league lead, the panicky people just might have started to get a little anxious.

And so Walter Alston had to get unconventional.

He picked Sandy Koufax to start yesterday afternoon's game at Ebbets Field against these same Cincinnati Reds. This was wholly unconventional, since Koufax had pitched only about 40 hours ago in a relief appearance, had not pitched for a month before that, and had not started a game since July 6th (also the only start of his young career).

Koufax would be facing a team that was in 5th place, but features the 2nd best hitting team in the National League behind only the Dodgers. And this Reds team came into the game having beaten Brooklyn 3 straight by scoring 18 runs.

The Reds' first 5 batters were all hitting .292 or better. The leadoff batter, Johnny Temple, flew out to Duke Snider in center. The 2nd batter, Smokey Burgess (.304 hitter), struck out. The 3rd batter, Ted Kluszewski, one of the most feared hitters in baseball with 41 home runs and a .314 average, hit a ground ball that went through for a single into right field. The 4th batter, Wally Post, also hitting .314 and with 32 home runs, flew out to Carl Furillo in right field.

Koufax had survived the top of the 1st inning.

In the bottom of the 1st, Sandy's battery mate, Roy Campanella provided immediate run support as he hit a sacrifice fly scoring Jim Gilliam from 3rd base. Then Carl Furillo followed that with a 2-run homer that sailed on a line drive into deep center field. It was the 22nd homer of the season for Skoonj.

Dodgers 3 Reds 0 – end of 1st inning

In the top of the 2nd, Koufax registered a 1-2-3 inning, striking out both Gus Bell (.309 hitter) and Rocky Bridges (.297 hitter).

In the 3rd it was another 1-2-3 inning, this time striking out Roy McMillan (.262 hitter) and the pitcher, Art Fowler.

In the 4th, Koufax gave up his 1st walk to the slugger Kluszewski, and that was all. He finished the inning by striking out Gus Bell for the 2nd time in this game, and the 3rd time he had faced him in 2 days.

The 5th inning was another 1-2-3 for Sandy including 2 more strikeouts.

In the 6th Sandy opened with his 9th strikeout, but then got into a jam when he walked two and had to face Big Klu. He got Kluszewski to fly out to Furillo in right. But then with Wally Post at the plate, Koufax was called for a balk. Now with Reds' runners on 2nd and 3rd and 2 outs, Koufax got out of the inning when Post flied to Furillo.

In the 7th, Koufax got Gus Bell on a strikeout for the 4th consecutive time. That's no small feat considering Bell was in the top 10 in batting in the National League as of last Sunday.

With 2 outs, Koufax again walked two Reds, but got out of it when Chuck Harmon struck out swinging. Sandy now had 11 K's.

A Jackie Robinson homer in the bottom of the 7th extended Koufax's lead to 7 – 0.

In the 8th, Koufax retired the side in order, notching two more strikeouts, the second one a swinging strikeout of Ted Kluszewski.

In the 9th, Koufax got Wally Post to ground out to Robinson at 3rd. Then he got Gus Bell swinging for his 4th strikeout facing Koufax today and 5th consecutive time in 2 days. This may be a record for consecutive strikeouts of a .300+ hitter by a single pitcher.

With 2 outs, Sam Mele came up. Mele, the veteran left fielder, nearing the end of his career, came into the game batting just .153, and was 0 for 3 with 1 strikeout. In this at bat he hit a line drive to left field and wound up on 2nd base with a double, just his 3rd of the season.

And with that hit, Mele became the 1st Reds' batter to get a base hit since Ted Kluszweski's single with 2 outs in the 1st inning.

Sandy Koufax had pitched 8 full innings of no-hit baseball.

Mele didn't last long on 2nd base. The next batter, Rocky Bridges hit a short fly that Pee Wee Reese grabbed to end the game.

Bonus baby Sandy Koufax had pitched a masterpiece. It was a 2-hit shutout with 14 strikeouts.

Today in the Newark Star-Ledger, John Craig wrote, ***"Sandy Koufax, a 19-year-old bonus kid, who only a year ago was sitting in the stands rooting for the Dodgers, came out of the oblivion of the bullpen today and turned in the club's most sensational performance of the season."***

Indeed Koufax's pitching performance was perhaps the 2nd most sensational in the National League so far this season. His 14 strikeouts were the National League high for a single game.

Sportswriters considered it to be 2nd best game pitched in the National League in 1955, behind only the incredible game pitched by another rookie, Sam "Toothpick" Jones of the Cubs, back on May 12th. He was called toothpick because he actually pitched with a toothpick hanging out of his mouth. In the May 12th game, Jones entered the 9th inning at Wrigley Field needing 3 outs for a no-hitter against the Pirates. Toothpick immediately traipsed into trouble. He walked 3 straight Pirates to load the bases. Not only was his no-hitter in jeopardy, but so was the game with the Cubs leading 4 – 0 and the tying run at the plate.

Jones proceeded to strike out the next batter, Dick Groat on 3 straight curve balls that Groat never swung at. Next up was another rookie, Roberto Clemente. He lunged at the first 2 pitches. At 0 and 2 he fouled off 2 pitches, and then he struck out swinging. With 2 outs the batter was slugger Frank Thomas. Thomas worked the count at 1 and 2, Jones threw a high curve for a called strike 3. The game was over. Jones had pitched a no-hitter.

NOTE from The Sports Time Traveler

Toothpick Jones became the 1st African-American pitcher to throw a no-hitter in major league baseball history.

In the 9th inning, the 3 players he struck out had deep resumes. Dick Groat won the NL MVP award in 1960 and was 2nd in MVP voting in 1963. Roberto Clemente won 4 batting titles, was the 1966 MVP, reached

3,000 hits and is a member of the Hall of Fame. And Frank Thomas, went on to hit 286 home runs in a 16 year career.

Now back to 1955.

Coming back to Koufax, the shutout took his ERA for the season down to a stellar 1.31, easily the best on the Dodgers staff. It was also the best ERA in the entire major leagues. But Sandy's name wasn't at the top of the list in the New York Times list of pitchers today, since he didn't have the minimum 75 innings pitched. Koufax had pitched just 20 innings all year through yesterday's game.

Roy Campanella, who caught the game, told Ross McGowen in the New York Times today, ***"He had a real good curve, and his fastball was good too. His control was alright. He was never wild at any time. Didn't ever miss the plate by much."***

Koufax had at least 1 strikeout in every inning in posting his 14 strikeouts, which are the most recorded by a pitcher in the National League this year.

In today's Cincinnati Enquirer, Reds beat writer Lou Smith predicted that Koufax, ***"can't miss blossoming into one of the game's brightest pitching stars. He has poise, a smooth delivery, along with a changeup that usually takes years for a youngster to acquire."***

Smith also explained to his Ohio readers why Koufax was passed over by the Reds who had scouted him when he was pitching last year for the University of Cincinnati freshman baseball team. Smith wrote that Koufax, ***"failed to impress the Cincinnati scouts, who reported that along with being wild, he didn't have major league stuff."***

The Sports Time Traveler will continue following the 1955 Dodgers as they try to officially wrap up the National League pennant race.

Chapter Fifteen

The 4th Place Team Is the Favorite

The Boston Red Sox are in 4th place in the American League with under 20 games remaining, yet they may be in the driver's seat for the 1955 pennant

FENWAY PARK, BOSTON - September 7, 1955

The Sports Time Traveler is following the 1955 Dodgers. The Dodgers were off yesterday. They lead the NL by 15 games and their magic number is down to 3 with 18 games to play.

The question is not whether the Dodgers will reach their 5th World Series in the past 8 years, but rather who will they play.

It's a fascinating question, because in the American League they've got one of the closest races in history. Last year's AL champion Indians lead the perennial favorite Yankees by just a half game. Just 1 game further back are the White Sox, who haven't been to the World Series since the 1919 Black Sox scandal.

But just another 1.5 games back (3 games out of 1st place) are the most intriguing team of the bunch - The Boston Red Sox.

Here are the standings as of "this morning" September 7, 1955

83 - 54 Indians

82 - 54 Yankees

81 - 55 White Sox

79 - 56 Red Sox

The Red Sox got off to a horrid start to the season. On Friday, May 27th they lost 16 - 0 at home at Fenway Park to the Washington Senators! And that dropped the Red Sox to 11 games out of 1st place with a 17 - 24 record.

The next day was the first game of the season played by Ted Williams. Williams had retired after the 1954 season, but decided to return.

The Splendid Splinter homered in his 1st at bat out of retirement, and although the Red Sox lost the game, Williams's return led to a Red Sox resurgence.

Williams himself was batting well over .400 in July before settling back to .352 as of "yesterday" (September 6, 1955).

The Red Sox have the best record in baseball at 62 - 32 since the day Ted Williams returned.

By comparison, the Yankees have been just 54 - 42 over that stretch. And even the Dodgers, who far and away have the best record in baseball this season, have only been 61 - 36 in the time since Ted Williams returned.

And here's the most fascinating part, as we get into the thick of this tight pennant race, the Red Sox have an overwhelming advantage.

Take a look at the home-away games left for each of the top 4 teams in the AL:

Indians - 3 home / 14 away

Yankees - 11 home / 7 away

White Sox - 5 home / 13 away

Red Sox - 16 home / 3 away

IF every team wins all their home games and loses all their away games, the final standings will look like this:

95 - 59 Red Sox

93 - 61 Yankees

86 - 68 White Sox

86 - 68 Indians

And that would put the Red Sox in the World Series for the first time since 1946. And it would create an incredible storyline for Ted Williams.

WORLD SERIES SCHEDULE

Yesterday baseball commissioner Ford Frick announced the World Series will begin on September 28. But if there is a tie in the AL, the alternate date will be September 29.

In the AL, a tie by 2 teams would necessitate a 1 game playoff, unlike the NL, which requires a best-of-3 playoff, the last of which led to the famous Bobby Thomson "Shot Heard Round the World" in the decisive game 3 victory by the Giants over the Dodgers 4 years ago in 1951.

But with this incredibly close pennant race, there is the specter of a 3-way or even a 4-way tie. And the AL announced yesterday they will be discussing the details of how that would be resolved.

The real possibility of the Red Sox climbing from 4th to 1st was discussed yesterday in an AP article by Joe Reichler. With the Red Sox winning 5 games in a row and having that massive home park advantage he wrote ***"The American League pennant race today swung to the Boston Red Sox."***

How serious of a threat are the Red Sox to win the pennant? The Yankees sent their top "spies" to Fenway Park. This was reported in a FRONT PAGE article in the Boston Globe.

The Sports Time Traveler will be following the conclusion of the 1955 season over the next few weeks.

Chapter Sixteen

A Penchant for Pennant Clinching

On September 8, 1955 the Brooklyn Dodgers had an opportunity to close out their 5th National League crown in 8 years, and do it earlier than any team in history

CHICAGO - September 10, 1955

The Sports Time Traveler embarked on a journey back in March to follow the 1955 Brooklyn Dodgers day-by-day.

Today, the Dodgers are in Chicago. But this story begins 2 days ago, and 90 miles north in Milwaukee.

September 8, 1955, presented the biggest opportunity of the season so far. The Dodgers were at County Stadium, knowing a victory against the 2nd place Milwaukee Braves would clinch the pennant.

The Dodgers opened the game facing Braves' starter, Bob Buhl. Buhl got the first 2 Dodgers out. But then he had to face Brooklyn's fearsome 3, 4 and 5 batters - all 3 of whom are in the top 5 in batting in the NL.

Buhl, apparently was afraid to pitch to this group and what followed was a base on balls bonanza.

First he walked Duke Snider (who has hit 42 HRs).

Then he hit Roy Campanella (32 HRs) on the wrist.

And he followed that up by walking Carl Furillo (47 extra-base hits).

With the bases loaded, he issued yet another base-on-balls to Jackie Robinson, scoring Snider with the 1st run of the game.

Next up, Gil Hodges drilled a single to drive in two Carl's! Carl Erskine, who was running for Campy, and Carl Furillo. Erskine had to replace Campy on the basepaths. Campy's wrist, which had been hit by Buhl's pitch, required ice packs be applied immediately, forcing him to exit the game. But no need for concern. The injury is just a bruise.

Moments later, Don Zimmer singled to drive in Jackie with the 4th run of the 1st inning. But by this time Buhl was already in the bathroom showers.

Later in the game, the Dodgers put up 6 more runs to win it easily 10 - 2.

Rookie pitchers Roger Craig and Karl Spooner combined to give up just 6 hits with Spooner getting the official credit for the victory, even though Craig left the game in the 4th inning with the lead.

When Spooner got the Braves' Del Rice to strike out swinging to end the contest, the Brooklyn Dodgers were League champions for the 12th time in franchise history and the 5th time in the past 8 years.

And the Dodgers did it earlier than they've ever done it before, in fact earlier than any National League team has ever clinched the pennant.

The New York Daily News, which reserves the back page for sports headlines, and real news for the front page, did something I've never seen before. They devoted the banner headlines on BOTH the front and back page to the Dodgers.

Here were the standings as of the morning of September 9, 1955:

92 – 46 Dodgers

76 – 64 Braves

72 – 66 Giants

72 – 69 Phillies

68 – 75 Redlegs

67 – 75 Cubs

57 – 80 Cardinals

55 – 84 Pirates

Just 11 days earlier the Braves were only 10 games out. But starting August 27, the Dodgers went on an 11 - 1 run, while the Braves won just 4 of 12 games.

It's almost poetic that this Dodgers' team, that started the season going on two consecutive 11 - 1 runs, should go on a 3rd 11 - 1 stretch to clinch the pennant.

NO ON FIELD CELEBRATION

Yet, there was no player celebration on the field when the clinching game concluded.

Roscoe McGowen in a rare FRONT PAGE story in the New York Times today described how the Dodgers reacted after the final strike, ***"There was no particular demonstration by the Dodgers on the field after the final out."***

John Craig, writing in the Newark Star-Ledger was in the clubhouse after the game and noted, ***"It was one of the quietest pennant celebrations ever."***

The lack of player enthusiasm for this achievement was likely due to the fact that the next step, winning a World Series, is something that has forever eluded the Brooklyn Dodgers.

"Dem Bums" have never won a World Series.

In particularly frustrating fashion, the Dodgers have lost to the Yankees in each of their prior 5 trips to the Fall Classic in 1941, 1947, 1949, 1952 and 1953.

And the captain of the team, Pee Wee Reese, has been the starting shortstop in all 5 of those World Series losses to their cross-borough rivals from the Bronx.

In the clubhouse after the game, Jack Lang of the Jersey Journal reported, ***"The Dodgers tried to whoop it up for the television and news reels. It was a little difficult for the Brooks to get real excited for this was a pennant they knew they had wrapped up long ago and the 10 - 2 clincher over the Braves was anticlimactic.***

HORSING AROUND GOES AWRY

There was no champagne in the locker room, only beer, and Jack Lang noted that the Dodgers weren't all that excited, ***"But they had to act excited*** (for the cameras) ***and started horsing around."***

Dion Henderson of the Madison, Wisconsin Capital Times wrote, ***"Don Zimmer began a campaign of destroying bats."*** And several other Dodgers joined in the shenanigans.

Lang reported that Duke Snider, added beer to the boyish bashing. He poured a can of beer on Don Newcombe's straw hat.

Newk wasn't happy about that or the teasing about his suddenly sorry looking hat that followed and the big man stormed off and left the odd locker room revelry.

There was some speculation that Newk was already miffed at not getting the start in the pennant clinching game. And if that was the case it would be understandable.

Newk, after all, has the best record of any starting pitcher in baseball at 20 - 4, and he tops the National League batting list for all players with 100+ at bats.

But the notion that Newk was feeling neglected wasn't borne out by beat writer Harvey Aronson's account in Newsday. He noted the glee exhibited by big Newk immediately after the game. In Aronson's story of the game, Newk was the 1st of the Dodgers to romp into the clubhouse. Aronson wrote, ***"The Ebbets Field idols had streamed into the locker room with a dazzling variety of triumphant yells. 'San Antone!' shouted Don Newcombe."***

But Jack Lang did observe that, ***"Newcombe angrily took a swipe at Duke Snider with his summer straw hat after the Duke had ruined the chapeau by soaking it with beer."***

THE PARTY FINALLY GETS GOING

After Newk stormed out, the mood improved. And a bit of a party got going when the team went to one of Milwaukee's German restaurants and consumed large quantities of champagne.

Partying then continued on the 2 hour charter bus ride to Chicago, where the Dodgers had to play a doubleheader yesterday. Lang called it, ***"the wildest, wettest bus trip in history. Champagne and liquor were taken aboard the buses and the boys really whooped it up."***

A MOST DREADFUL DODGERS DOUBLEHEADER... FOR 14 INNINGS

It's unclear if Newk was part of the dinner, or the mobile merriment on the bus trip, but yesterday at Wrigley Field, in a game that started less than 20 hours after the clincher ended, he pitched like he was seriously hungover.

Newk had his worst outing of the season in a totally meaningless affair.

He gave up a home run on his 1st pitch of the game, and then 2 more homers before he even got the 2nd man out. It was a 5 run 1st inning. Newk only lasted 2 innings and the Dodgers lost 11 - 4.

In the 2nd game of the doubleheader, the Dodgers were down 4 - 1 going into the 6th.

And then they somehow suddenly sobered up.

Over the final four frames they scored an unbelievable 15 runs, and took the nightcap 16 - 9.

The 15 runs in the last 4 innings, were more than the Dodgers scored in any game the entire season!

And this Dodgers' team has had a fantastic season at the plate. The Dodgers have 811 runs scored, while no other team has exceeded even 700 runs.

THE RED SOX THROW AWAY THEIR CHANCES

The question of who the Dodgers will play in the World Series has effectively been whittled down to 3 teams.

Just a few days ago I reported to you how the 4th place Boston Red Sox had made a spectacular run to get within 3 games of the league leading Indians. And with most of their games at Fenway for the remainder of the campaign, the Red Sox seemed to be in the driver's seat.

But the Red Sox have now lost their last 3 games including one in which they literally threw the game away, with the winning run scoring on a wild pitch.

Now the Red Sox are 6 games back with just 15 to play, and even with 12 of the 15 to be played at home, it's a tall order to leap over 3 other teams from that far behind.

That leaves the White Sox, Yankees and the Indians as the teams left to battle for the American League title.

KINER'S LAST DRIVE

Right now, the Indians hold the advantage with a 1.5 game lead over the Bronx Bombers. And a lot of the credit has to go to Ralph Kiner.

I didn't even know the former Pirates' legend, the man for whom the left field corner in Forbes Field is named, ever played for the Indians.

But yesterday he hit a homer to break a tie game in the 7th inning in Boston and the Indians went on to beat the Red Sox 3 - 1.

Then today, he hit a double and scored the 1st run of the game, and later his 2-run homer broke open the game as the Indians again downed the Red Sox 10 - 7.

Kiner, with 18 home runs and 54 RBIs in 108 games, is a major reason the Indians are looking like they can repeat as American League champions and make a bid to win the World Series that they lost in embarrassing fashion last year when the Giants swept them after Cleveland had a historic 111 - 43 regular season record.

And yet, no matter what happens down the stretch, Ralph Kiner, the man who won 7 consecutive home run titles in the National League, is adamant that this will be his last season in the majors.

By the way, Kiner's 7 consecutive home run titles with Pittsburgh, from 1946 - 1952, remains the longest streak ever in major league history. Not even the Babe ever won 7 consecutive league HR titles.

Here are the American League standings after the games from today, September 10, 1955:

87 – 54 Cleveland Indians

85 – 55 New York Yankees

83 – 57 Chicago White Sox

80 – 59 Boston Red Sox

71 – 70 Detroit Tigers

58 – 82 Kansas City A's

49 – 88 Washington Senators

44 – 92 Baltimore Orioles

The Sports Time Traveler will continue following the 1955 season and reporting to you when there is something so exciting I just have to share it.

Chapter Seventeen

Big KLU

Ted Kluszewski makes baseball history in 1955 and almost no one knows about it

I am taking a break from the 1955 Dodgers to share a story about Ted Kluszewski of the Cincinnati Reds.

His nickname was "BIG KLU."

Almost no baseball fans outside of Cincinnati mention his name anymore.

He's not in the Hall of Fame.

Yet all baseball fans should know about him.

He was famous here in the 1950s as the player who went sleeveless. His biceps were so big he couldn't fit into a Reds' uniform.

He's not so famous for something he did in 1955 that should be celebrated, but was unnoticed at the time, and is under appreciated back in our present time.

When the 1955 baseball season ended, BIG KLU achieved something no one else has done in the history of baseball. BIG KLU completed his 3rd consecutive season in which he hit 40+ home runs while striking out 40 or less times. And by the way, he batted at least .314 in each of those 3 seasons (1953 - 1955).

Think about that.

You don't have to strike out nearly 200 times to hit 40 homers. You can be a contact hitter. In the 2025 season, no player with 40+ home runs struck out less than 124 times.

Wouldn't it be nice if we had ballplayers like BIG KLU in the present time? A player who puts the ball in play and also can hit it into the bleachers. In each of those 3 seasons, Ted Kluszewski knocked in well over 100 runs, including a league leading 141 in 1954.

The incredible thing is that no newspapers here in 1955 mentioned BIG KLU's great accomplishment. Of course ballplayers didn't strike out with the frequency they do in the present time. Willie Mays led the majors with 51 homers in 1955 and struck out only 60 times. Mickey Mantle led the American League with 37 home runs and struck out 97 times.

But even so, what BIG KLU did deserved some attention. And yet it received none that I can find.

So here's to celebrating Ted Kluszweski, BIG KLU, on one of the greatest 3 season runs in the history of our national pastime.

POSTSCRIPT

Back in the present time, after I originally posted this story in my newsletter, The Sports Time Traveler, I heard from another player with the initials "TK," my friend Ted Kubiak.

Ted Kubiak played 10 years in the majors and was a key player on all 3 of the Oakland A's back-to-back-to-back World Series Championship teams in 1972, 1973 and 1974.

Ted Kubiak, who grew up following the Yankees in the 1950s, had this to say about Ted Kluszewski, ***"I knew of Kluszweski but because he got little play in the press, my only reminder of who he was were the size of his arms. That got more play that what he did on the field, and to tell you the truth, I had no idea he had the kind of years you mentioned. It's a shame because those were years that few players had, but he wasn't a big name on the East Coast and the Reds were never in contention for anything, so he got lost in the shuffle."***

Ted Kubiak then shared his thoughts about players like Kluszewski vs. power hitters today, "***no one works at the game like they should anymore, like they used to, and that is being accepted. Klu was a very good player in an era that expected more.***"

By the way, Ted Kubiak also famously scored the winning run in the 11th inning of game 3 of the 1973 World Series against the Mets. In my book, "The 1973 Mets - You've Got to Believe," I assert that Ted's heads up baserunning play that led to the winning run, was the key moment that enabled the A's to take the World Series, because the Mets pitchers shut down the A's in games 4 and 5 to take a 3 games to 2 lead. Had Ted not scored that winning run in the 11th inning, the Mets, playing at home, and with more players left on the bench, most likely would have won the game and went on to win the 1973 World Series 4 games to 1.

Chapter Eighteen

The World Series for Breakfast - A Preview of the Fall Classic

It's the Yankees vs. the Dodgers in the Fall Classic for the 5th time in 8 years, and the games are all on color TV at 8:45am on the West Coast

NEW YORK - Tuesday, September 28, 1955

The Sports Time Traveler has been following the 1955 baseball season daily since spring training. The regular season has now concluded and the World Series is scheduled to begin this afternoon at Yankee Stadium at 1pm ET.

The Series will be televised nationally in color (for those who have color TV sets). On the West Coast, many baseball fans will be able to watch the Yankees and the Dodgers while they eat breakfast.

The TV schedule for the entire World Series was displayed in the Fresno Bee in California this morning. The broadcast starting times for all the games is 8:45am.

When I first saw the air times of 8:45am, I thought perhaps they were going to have a very long pre-game show. But then I found out that's not the case. Several California newspapers mentioned the pre-game show was just 15 minutes and game time would be 9am PST.

I did a little investigating and found out that here in 1955, the entire west coast (California, Oregon and Washington) set the clocks back to standard time on September 25th, while most of the rest of the country are still on daylight savings time until the end of October.

As a result, the west coast is 4 hours behind New York for the next month. Personally, I found this fascinating. And for baseball fans in the west, the games will almost certainly all be finished well before noon. It's going to be the World Series for breakfast each day.

Tickets for $2 in Yankee Stadium

For fans in New York who want to go to Yankee Stadium to see game 1 live today, tickets are still available in the outfield bleachers. They will be on sale at 8am ET at a price of $2.10 each. A crowd of well over 60,000 is expected in the stadium today as the giant ballpark has a capacity of 67,000.

No Seats Available for Game 3 in Ebbets Field

In contrast, when the series moves cross-town to Ebbets Field in Brooklyn for game 3, no tickets will be available as the tiny "band-box" park seats only 34,000 and is already sold out.

Should All the World Series Games Be Played in One of the Larger New York Stadiums?

With only half the seating capacity of cavernous Yankee Stadium, and only 60% of the seating capacity of the Polo Grounds, many New Yorkers have questioned whether the series games should be played at Ebbets Field at all.

On August 2nd, a shocking article by Dick Young appeared in the New York Daily News in which Dodgers' owner, Walter O'Malley, indicated he might favor playing World Series games in a larger New York ballpark. The headline of the story read, ***"O'Malley Favors Shift From EF for Series."***

Following up on the O'Malley article, on August 13th, when the Dodgers had a 15 game lead in National League, The New York Daily News shared letters from readers who were responding to a question the Daily News had posed about the World Series venue, ***"Would you like to see the Brooklyn Dodgers play their World Series games at the Polo Grounds or Yankee Stadium instead of Ebbets Field?"***

While the topic may seemingly have sounded heretical to die-hard Dodgers fans, the small sample size of Dodgers fans' responses published in the Daily News favored the Dodgers moving their World Series games to one of the bigger New York ballparks.

Here were a few of the responses from *DODGERS FANS*:

Jack Casertano, a truck driver said, ***"Yes, I have no objection whatsoever to Yankee Stadium or the Polo Grounds. Wherever the Dodgers play they'll win the series... I'd like to rub it into the Yankees by beating them in their own ballpark."***

Leonard W. Young, a chauffeur said, ***"Ebbets Field can't accommodate the number of fans that want to see the series... I'm one of those who support the Dodgers all year. I've never been able to get a World Series ticket."***

Jimmy Walkes, a superintendent, said, ***"It would be great to see the Dodgers play their games at Yankee Stadium... It's a ballpark not a band box like Ebbets Field."***

Ultimately, no serious discussion took place about moving the World Series games away from Ebbets Field.

Practice at the Other Team's Park

One oddity of the subway series is that each team had an opportunity to practice at the other team's park.

Yesterday, the Yankees practiced at Ebbets Field. 2nd baseman Billy Martin showed his contempt for the tiny ballpark referring to it as ***"a cracker box,"*** according to Joseph Sheehan of the New York Times. Ebbets has some of the shortest fences in the majors, with straightaway centerfield at just 393 feet. This helped the Dodgers become the only team in baseball this year to hit over 200 home runs. They hit 119 of their 201 home runs at home at Ebbets Field.

The 165 pound Martin, who hit just 1 home run all season, blasted a ball into the left field stands in one of his first swings.

Jim McCulley of the Daily News reported, ***"The Yankees were again amazed by the short fences in Flatbush."***

Meanwhile at Yankee Stadium, where the Dodgers were working out, the team focused mostly on fielding. Game 1 starter Don Newcombe reportedly worked out harder than any of the other Dodgers' players. McCulley noted that Newk, ***"spent almost an hour running. He did wind sprints from 11:45 to 12:30 to get himself in top physical condition."***

The Mick Might Miss the Series

The biggest news from the practice sessions is that Mickey Mantle is unlikely to play in the World Series. The Mick tore a muscle in the back of his right thigh last week. He now has a blood clot, and he can't run. He told Joe Trimble of the New York Daily News, ***"I'm not hopeful of playing in the series - at least in the first two at the Stadium."***

Taking Mantle's place in center field will be Irv Noren, the Yankees regular left fielder. Noren hit .253 this year with 8 home runs. Mantle in contrast hit .306 and led the American League with 37 home runs. Mantle, striking fear in opposing pitchers, also drew a league leading 113 walks, which gave him an American League best .431 On Base Percentage, 100 points higher than Noren.

Starting in the other outfield positions for the Yankees will be Hank Bauer in right field and a rookie, Elston Howard, in left field.

Today will be the first time in Yankees history that in the 1st game of a World Series they don't have in their outfield either Babe Ruth, Joe DiMaggio or Mickey Mantle.

Oddsmaker Predictions

Despite missing Mantle, the oddsmakers have installed the Yankees as a 13 - 10 favorite to win the World Series.

Perhaps there is a feeling that no matter who puts on the pinstripes, the Bronx Bombers will still defeat "Dem Bums."

The Yankees have beaten the Dodgers every time they've faced off in the Fall Classic - in 1941, 1947, 1949, 1952 and 1953.

The Dodgers have NEVER won a World Series title in their franchise history. They are 0 for 7 in prior World Series appearances.

The Yankees have won the Fall Classic 16 times in their franchise history. And since 1927, the Yankees have won 15 of the 16 times they've been to the World Series, losing only during the war in 1942.

National Sportswriters Concur - The Yankees Will Win

An AP poll of 49 baseball sportswriters this week found that 31 pick the Yankees to win the World Series over the Dodgers. 2 of the writers pick the Yankees in a sweep.

Al Wolf of The Los Angeles Times explained the strong sentiment towards the Yankees is due to the history books, ***"The Yanks are favorites simply from force of habit. They have played in 20 World Series and won 16 of them, the last seven in succession... The Dodgers have never triumphed in seven tries."***

Wolf also noted that Dodgers' ace Don Newcombe has not beaten the Yankees in the World Series, losing the first and fourth games in 1949.

NOTE: Newcombe was serving in the Korean War and didn't play in the 1952 and 1953 World Series against the Yankees.

YANKEES - Finished the Season Like Champions

Another factor favoring the Yankees is that they finished the season like champions.

After leading the American League by a small margin most of the summer, the Yankees had relinquished the top spot to the Chicago White Sox at the end of August, and found themselves locked in a heated 4-team battle in September.

On September 13th, the Yanks were 2 games behind the defending league champion Cleveland Indians.

The Yankees proceeded to win 8 straight and 10 of their final 12 to lock up the pennant. Thus, the Yankees come into the series as a hot team.

DODGERS - September Swoon

In contrast, the Dodgers, who had one of the greatest starts in major league history at 22 - 2, and clinched the National League pennant earlier than any team ever on September 8th, had nothing left to play for in the final 3 weeks of the season and experienced a September swoon, winning just 6 of their final 16 games.

The Boston Globe's, Roger Birtwell, penned a piece in which he posed the question, ***"Will the 1955 Dodgers be like the Red Sox of '46?"*** He went on to explain, ***"Both made a stampede of the early stages of the race. The '46 Red Sox won 21 of their first 24 games. The '55 Dodgers won 21 of their first 23... and during the last third of the season neither club did very well."***

The point of the piece, as all readers in Boston surely knew (and so it wasn't stated) is that the Red Sox lost the 1946 World Series, and clearly Birtwell thinks things don't bid well for Dem Bums here in '55.

DODGERS - Slumping Stars and Sore Arms

But even more concerning about the Dodgers is that their two superstars during the first two-thirds of the season, when they built their insurmountable National League lead, Duke Snider and Don Newcombe, both finished the season poorly.

On August 5th, when Snider hit 2 homers to reach 38 for the season, there was serious talk about him challenging Babe Ruth's hallowed record of 60 for a single season. The Duke had reached 38 in 108 games and that was 7 games AHEAD of Ruth's pace, as the Babe had not reached 38 homers until his 115th game.

In addition, Snider was a legitimate triple crown threat, leading the league in home runs and RBIs, and was 3rd in batting average. In the rivalry among great New York center fielders between Willie, Mickey and the Duke (Willie Mays of the Giants, Mickey Mantle of the Yankees and Duke Snider of the Dodgers), the Duke was clearly at the top in the summer of 1955.

Meanwhile Don Newcombe was having a sensational and unprecedented season. On August 1st, Newcombe had a record of 18 - 1 with a 2.95 ERA. Only one other pitcher had ever started a season with a better record through their first 19 decisions. Rube Marquad had started 19 - 0 for the Giants in 1912.

But Marquard had not done what Newk had at the plate. Marquard was a better than average hitter for a pitcher, and was hitting .220 when he won his 19th game.

But Newk was simply hitting off the charts in 1955. On August 1st, Don Newcombe had a batting average of .384. And that was good enough to lead the National League for all batters with more than 85 at bats.

Yet both Duke and Newk had meltdowns over the last 6 weeks of the campaign. Snider hit just 4 homers after August 5th to finish with 42. And he hit only .279 in September.

Newk, who looked like he could have become the first pitcher since Dizzy Dean in 1934 to win 30 games, had a record of just 2 - 4 in the final 2 months of the season. He developed a sore arm in September and had to miss a couple of starts and did not look sharp in any outing after mid-August.

In addition, several other Dodgers' pitchers have sore arms as well. One of them, Carl Erskine, beat the Yankees in game 3 of the 1953 World Series with a record 14 strikeouts. But Dodgers' manager, Walter Alston, believes he can perhaps get 1 game out of Erskine's arm in the 1955 series and that will force Alston to use some of his younger pitchers who are untested on the World Series stage.

One sportswriter, John Fox, sports editor of the Binghamton Press, suggested that the Dodgers should give 19-year-old Sandy Koufax an opportunity to pitch in the series. Koufax, whose contract bonus size required him to be on the Dodgers' roster, per league rules, started 5 games for the Dodgers and 2 of them were gems, a 2-hit, 14 strikeout shutout on August 27th and a 5-hit shutout on September 3rd.

But as Fox noted, Alston has already wasted Koufax's gifted left arm by having him pitch 2 days of heavy batting practice trying to simulate the Yankees' expected lefty starters Whitey Ford and Tommy Byrne that the Dodgers' will see in games 1 and 2.

DODGERS Advantages

The Dodgers do have some potential major advantages.

The Dodgers are loaded with right-handed power. 138 of their major league leading 201 homers were hit by righties. The right-handed domination was so strong that National League teams rarely pitched lefties against the Dodgers. During 1955, only 8% of all Dodgers' at bats were against left-handed pitchers. And the Dodgers had a .536 slugging % against those lefties vs. .440 vs. righties.

So clear was the adage that you can't pitch lefties against the Dodgers that the Milwaukee Braves held out Warren Spahn, one of the greatest lefty pitchers in history, and in the prime of his career in 1955, from pitching a single inning against the Dodgers in 1955. Spahn pitched in 39 games in 1955, totaling at least 3 against every one of the 6 other clubs. But he never pitched against the Brooklyn Dodgers in 1955.

The Yankees have a conundrum, since their best starting pitchers, Whitey Ford and Tommy Byrne are lefties. This is a seemingly huge advantage for Brooklyn. However the crafty Yankees' manager, Casey Stengel, plans to start Ford and Byrne in games 1 and 2 at Yankee Stadium, where he expects the righty power of the Dodgers will be neutralized by the vast distances of the left field fences in Yankee Stadium.

The other Dodger advantage is simple run production. Brooklyn was the only team in the majors to average more than 5 runs per game at 5.6. The Yankees averaged 4.9.

The Dodgers' number 3, 4, 5 and 6 batters pose a more fearsome group than any other team in baseball can put together. Take a look at their stats:

HRs	**RBIs**	**Avg**	
42	**136**	**.309**	**Duke Snider**
32	**107**	**.318**	**Roy Campanella**
26	**95**	**.314**	**Carl Furillo**
27	**102**	**.289**	**Gil Hodges**

And the Dodgers also have the best pinch-hitter in baseball in, wait for it... Don Newcombe. That's right, their ace pitcher was also the major leagues' best pinch-hitter in 1955. Newcombe batted .381 as a pinch-hitter.

Another Dodgers advantage is that all 7 World Series games will be played during the day. The Dodgers for whatever reason, are a better day game team than night game team. In fact, the Dodgers were downright mediocre at night this season with a record of just 32 – 31. But during the day, the Dodgers dominated with a record of 66 – 24. The Dodgers daytime advantage was a batting bonanza during the day when the team hit .284. At night they collectively cooled off to .252. In individual player terms, that's the difference between being sent down to the minors, versus having a starting position penciled in for next year.

In contrast, the Yankees were better at night with a 29 – 16 record. Their 67 – 42 daytime record was over 100 percentage points worse than the Dodgers.

The Dodgers have one more intangible advantage in the multi-talented Jackie Robinson that was pointed out by Harry Grayson, sports editor of the Newspaper Enterprise Association in his syndicated article, ***"To beat the Yankees, the Dodgers must have a conflagration lit under them, and if he can get on base, the fading but still fiery Robinson is the old boy to apply the torch."***

It's going to be a fascinating World Series. Game 1 is today. As The Sports Time Traveler I will be listening to the radio broadcast of the game and reading the stories in the papers tomorrow.

I can't wait!

Chapter Nineteen

1955 World Series Game 1 – Sealing or Stealing the Series

Both the Yankees and the Dodgers made bold moves in an effort to take the early command of the series

YANKEE STADIUM - September 29, 1955

Yesterday afternoon the 1955 World Series opened between the Yankees and the Dodgers. It's 5th time in 8 years these two clubs have faced off. The Yankees have won every time. And the Yankees have won the World Series 15 times in their last 16 appearances going back to 1927. The Dodgers have never won a World Series, losing all 7 times they won the National League pennant.

But the Dodgers have reason to believe this year can be different. They had the most potent offense in all of baseball this year. They were the only team to slug more than 200 home runs. And they were the only team to average more than 5 runs per game.

In addition, the Dodgers had the best hitter in baseball this year, who also happens to be their ace starting pitcher. Don Newcombe had a 20 - 5 record and batted .359, although he didn't qualify for the batting title with just 125 plate appearances.

The Dodgers also match up well against their cross-town rivals. The Yankees two best starting pitchers are lefty. And this presents a conundrum for Yanks' manager Casey Stengel, as all National League teams knew this year, you can't pitch lefties against this Dodgers team that is loaded with right-handed sluggers. Even the legendary Warren Spahn of the Milwaukee Braves, one of the best lefty pitchers in history, who won 17 games in 1955 against the rest of the NL clubs, was held out against the Dodgers, never pitching to a single Dodgers batter in 22 games between the clubs this season.

The Mick is Out

Making matters worse for the Yankees, their best hitter, 23 year old superstar center fielder Mickey Mantle, is out with a torn muscle. Mantle led the Yankees in hits and runs scored. He led the entire American League in home runs, triples, walks, slugging percentage and on-base percentage. His replacement, Irv Noren, batted just .253.

Missing Mantle is a big blow to the Bronx Bombers.

And Mickey is not out just for game 1. Dana Mozley of the New York Daily News reported this morning, ***"Mantle probably won't play in the series."***

NOTE from The Sports Time Traveler

Before beginning the coverage of game 1, I've come back to the present to share a quick story about my dad. Eight years earlier, prior to game 1 of the 1947 World Series also between the Yankees and the Dodgers, my dad was in elementary school and he had a conundrum. All the games were

scheduled to be played in the daytime. And game 1 was on a Tuesday, so my dad had to be in school.

My dad got up the guts to ask his mom if he could stay home to watch the World Series. Of course, his mother (my grandmother) Estelle, a stern disciplinarian, told my dad he was not going to miss school. My dad lamented that he was going to miss the game completely since the school will not let kids bring radios. My grandmother did a little thinking. She was the president of the PTA so she decided to talk to the principal.

At the principal's office, my grandmother made the appeal to allow students to bring radios. The principal thought about it and said, *"Well, the Dodgers haven't been to the World Series since before the war."* **The principal decided to allow the students to bring radios. And so my dad got to listen to the 1947 World Series during school.**

Now back to 1955 and the beginning of game 1 of the 1955 World Series.

First Ball Thrown Is a Strike

New York City mayor Robert Wagner threw the ceremonial first pitch of the 1955 World Series. The former Yale baseball manager made it a perfect strike to Yankees' catcher Yogi Berra.

As the game began, Yankees' ace Whitey Ford got Jim Gilliam to hit a grounder right back to him for the 1st out of the series. But the 2nd batter, Pee Wee Reese slashed a ball over the head of his shortstop counterpart, Phil Rizzuto, into left field for a single and the 1st hit of the 1955 series.

This brought up the always dangerous Duke Snider for the 1st tense moment of the Fall Classic. Ford got 2 strikes on Snider and then got him swinging on a sweeping curve for out number 2. Next up, catcher Roy Campanella popped to Billy Martin at 2nd base and Whitey Ford had retired the side without a runner reaching 2nd base.

In the bottom of the 1st, the Yankees had a surprise for the Dodgers. Leadoff batter Hank Bauer bunted perfectly to the right of Don Newcombe, and reached 1st base safely. But Newk struck out the 2nd batter, 3rd baseman Gil McDougald, and got out of the inning when Mantle's replacement, Irv Noren, bounced a ball to Dodgers' 2nd baseman Don Zimmer, who turned it into an inning ending double play.

Both pitchers had navigated the top of the order without harm in the 1st.

Dodgers 0 Yankees 0 - end of the 1st inning

The potential for an old fashioned pitchers' duel evaporated on the 1st pitch of the 2nd inning. Dodgers' slugger Carl Furillo hit a "chip shot" that sliced toward the right field foul pole according to John Drebinger's front page article in the New York Times, ***"The ball struck the top of the four-foot railing between the first and second gates, about 300 feet away. It then bounced into the seats."***

It was a home run for Furillo to give Brooklyn the early lead at 1 - 0.

There was great irony in this home run for Brooklyn, because not only had the ball struck iron, landing on the railing, but it had also gone out of the playing field in the shallowest portion of the park. The right field line was just 296 feet from home plate in Yankee Stadium. And the fence, as mentioned by Drebinger, was just 4 feet high. Furillo had hit a ball that in any other park would have dropped into the field of play. Just a day earlier the Yankees, practicing in Ebbets Field, had been chiding the Dodgers for their tiny "band-box" ballpark. Now it was the Yankees' short porch that the Dodgers had leveraged for a home run to kick off the scoring.

Two batters later, the eccentric dimensions of old Yankee Stadium yielded another outlandish outcome. 36 year old Jackie Robinson, the Dodgers' 3rd baseman, took Whitey Ford deep... very deep. Drebinger wrote, ***"Robinson weighed in with a tremendous blast to left-center that traveled close to 440 feet... By the time the ball was returned to the infield Robbie was on third with a triple."***

The United Press play-by-play account of the game indicated Robinson's drive, ***"bounded onto the red cinder path near the 457-foot mark."***

It's interesting to note that Robinson's ball traveled a little to the left of the site where the monuments are located inside the playing field at Yankee Stadium. These three monuments, one to Babe Ruth (erected in 1949), one to Lou Gehrig (erected in 1941) and one to their Murderer's Row manager, Miller Huggins (erected in 1932), add yet another quirk to the vast left centerfield area.

Robinson would have had a home run in perhaps every other stadium, but in Yankee Stadium, it was just a very long base hit that the aging star legged out for a triple.

It is interesting to note however, that Ed Corrigan of the AP, thought that a younger Jackie would have made it into an inside-the-park homer. He wrote, ***"When Robinson hit his triple, it was painfully apparent how much he has slowed down. He had to slide to beat the throw. A couple of years ago he might have tried to stretch it to a home run."***

You can see both Furillo's homer and Robinson's blast in a one minute YouTube video by typing, "Game 1 1955 World Series Brooklyn Dodgers vs New York Yankees," into the YouTube search bar.

Robbed of a home run by the "Death Valley" in left field inside the House that Ruth Built, Jackie managed to score anyway just moments later when Don Zimmer hit a pop-fly to short center that dropped in for a single. And now the ace Ford had let up 2 runs on 3 hits and there was still only 1 out. The potential existed for a big inning with Don Newcombe coming to the plate. But Newk grounded out. And after issuing a walk to Jim Gilliam, Ford got Pee Wee Reese to hit a grounder that retired the side.

In the bottom of the 2nd, after Newk got Yogi Berra to ground out, he walked 1st baseman Joe Collins and then faced rookie left fielder, Elston Howard. Howard fouled off Don Newcombe's 1st pitch. On the 2nd pitch there was ***"a loud crack as Howard swung,"*** according to the INS reporter. The crack was Howard hammering a ball down the line in left field and 6 rows deep into the lower left field stands for a home run to tie the game at 2. The left field line was only 301 feet, so this was another short homer.

Imagine what Elston Howard must have felt like hitting a home run in his 1st World Series at bat. Fortunately one reporter from the International News Service did ask Howard. He said, ***"When I went up to bat I knew my wife was home watching me on television. She's a baseball fan but couldn't attend the game because we are expecting a baby next month. I was shaky standing up there. Never felt so nervous in a ballgame. That home run was the biggest thrill of my baseball career. It took all the nervousness out of me. After that it was just another ballgame to me."***

Now it was the Yankees with 2 runs in and just 1 out that had the potential for a big inning. But Newk got 2nd baseman Billy Martin to hit a fly to right and Phil Rizzuto to hit a grounder to Robinson at 3rd who threw to Hodges for the 3rd out.

Dodgers 2 Yankees 2 - end of the 2nd inning

The 3rd inning began similar to the 2nd inning with the 1st batter being another dangerous Dodgers' slugger, perhaps the most dangerous in the National League in 1955, the Duke.

But Snider came into the Fall Classic with a massive power outage. After being a week ahead of Babe Ruth's 60 home run pace on August 5th, Snider hit just 4 homers in his last 43 games, and none after September 5th.

And facing a lefty pitcher, Snider, as the one big lefty batter in the Dodgers' heavy right-handed hitting lineup, was at a tremendous disadvantage and had struck out in his first at bat.

However, Milton Richman of the UP described why the Duke was likely not distraught when he stepped into the batter's box against Ford for the 2nd time. Richman wrote, ***"Duke Snider was like a kid with a new toy before the ball game. Snider, who hadn't hit a home run for the Dodgers during the last two weeks of the season, was happy because he said, 'I found the range again,' during pre-game batting practice. The Duke proved it too, when***

he hammered one of Ford's third-inning serves high up into the right field stands, or what is commonly called Mickey Mantle territory."

Snider hit what Whitey Ford described as a hanging curve. And he crushed it. The ball landed in the 3rd tier of the right field stands, 10 rows deep. Unlike Furillo's Yankee Stadium gift homer, or Howard's drive down the line in left, the Duke's majestic drive was launched into the stratosphere of the stadium and would have been a homer in any ballpark in America. And it put the Dodgers back in front 3 - 2.

Ford got through the rest of the inning quite easily, striking out Jackie Robinson looking for the 3rd out.

In the bottom of the 3rd, Newcombe made a critical mistake when he walked pitcher Whitey Ford. Leadoff hitter Hank Bauer then singled, putting runners on 1st and 2nd with no outs. Then Newcombe got 3 successive Yankees to ground out. But Whitey Ford was able to move to 3rd base on the 1st groundout and he scored on the 2nd one to tie the game at 3.

Dodgers 3 Yankees 3 - end of the 3rd inning

In the top of the 4th, Zimmer led off with a walk and Newcombe tried to bunt him over, but the Yankees got Zimmer at 2nd. Ford then gave up another walk to Jim Gilliam to put runners on 1st and 2nd with 1 out. But Ford got out of the inning when he got Pee Wee Reese to hit a double play ball to Billy Martin at 2nd.

In the bottom of the 4th, Yankees' 1st baseman Joe Collins led off. The 32-year-old had been the regular 1st baseman since the middle of the 1951 season when he replaced the aging Hall of Famer Johnny Mize. Collins had been dependable but not exciting. His best year had been 1952, when he had 42 extra base hits and batted .280. But in 1955, he had slumped to just 23 extra base hits and batted a lowly .234. This was Collins's 4th World Series, and his track record batting in the Fall Classic had been abysmal. He had batted .222 in the 1951 series, .000 in 1952 and .167 in 1953.

In his 1st at bat in this game he walked. Now in his 2nd time facing Don Newcombe he slashed the 2nd pitch on a line drive that landed in the lower right field stands for a home run. Joe Collins had put the Yankees in front 4 - 3.

After Collins's homer, the Dodgers had an easy time in the inning. Newk got shortstop Phil Rizzuto, and Elston Howard to strikeout, and Campy threw out Billy Martin trying to steal 2nd base after he had singled.

Yankees 4 Dodgers 3 - end of the 4th inning

In the top of the 5th, Ford faced the heart of the Dodgers' order. Singles by Carl Furillo and Gil Hodges put runners on 1st and 3rd with 2 outs for Jackie Robinson. Jackie got good wood on a Ford pitch and hit it to deep center field. But it's nearly impossible for most batters to hit a homer to center field in Yankee Stadium with its 461 foot fence and Irv Noren made the catch to end the threat.

In the bottom of the 5th, Newk got the Yankees in order and the score remained 4 - 3 Yankees after 5.

Ford also had a 1-2-3 inning in the top of the 6th.

In the bottom of the 6th with 1 out and Yogi Berra on 1st base, Joe Collins came to the plate. Collins had homered in his last at bat, and this time he belted Newk again. The United Press called it, ***"a towering drive into the right field bleachers."***

Drebinger noted that the ball cleared the auxiliary scoreboard in right field. ***"Snider tearing over from center, made a great leaping try for it, but couldn't make it."*** The ball had traveled at least 400 feet. It was a 2-run shot and extended the Yankees' lead to 6 - 3.

Who needs Mickey Mantle when you have Joe Collins?

Casey Stengel sung praises for his 1st baseman after the game. He told Jim McCulley in the New York Daily News, ***"He has been a money player for me***

ever since I've known him... Collins, I think, right now is the best at first base in our league... I can't say enough for Collins."

After Collins's homer, Newk got Elston Howard to ground out for the 2nd out. Then Billy Martin hit a ball into left field that went over Jim Gilliam's head and rolled all the way to deep left field wall. Martin made it to 3rd base standing up.

That was enough for Dodgers' manager Walter Alston to take Newk out. The Dodgers' ace in 1955 had given up 6 runs in 5 and 2/3 innings.

Don Bessent, who had a sensational rookie season with an 8 - 1 record and a 2.70 ERA came in to relieve Newcombe.

Now with 2 outs, and Eddie Robinson pinch-hitting for Rizzuto, Billy Martin decided to try and steal home on the rookie pitcher's 2nd throw to the plate. This was not part of Casey Stengel's plans. Stengel told McCulley, ***"I was shocked when I saw Billy go for the plate. But he's that kind of player, aggressive."***

Bessent saw Martin and ***"whipped the ball in, Martin was out by a good 10 feet,"*** according to Jimmy Powers in the Daily News.

Campanella dove on top of Martin in applying the tag that ended the inning. Martin was peeved. Joe Trimble of the Daily News wrote, ***"Martin and Campy tangled angrily as Roy threw a bear hug around Billy. The Yankee fire eater jumped up angrily and wrestled himself free from the burly backstop."***

Yankees 6 Dodgers 3 - end of the 6th inning

Ford and Bessent both threw 1-2-3 innings in the 7th.

Carl Furillo led off the 8th inning with a single for his 3rd hit of the game. After Gil Hodges flied out, Jackie Robinson hit a bouncing ball to Gil McDougald at 3rd base that had inning ending potential. But the ball bounced off his knee and into left field and Furillo reached 3rd base and Robinson ended up on 2nd. Now the Dodgers had 2 runners in scoring position and the tying run at the plate in Don Zimmer. Zimmer hit a fly to deep left that scored Furillo and allowed Robinson to get to 3rd base. The score was now Yankees 6 Dodgers 4.

Now Alston sent in a pinch-hitter Frank Kellert for the pitcher Bessent. On the 2nd pitch to Kellert, Jackie Robinson broke for home. The Buffalo News reported that Robinson ***"stole the base cleanly, sliding in ahead of Ford's hurried throw."***

Bob Whiting of the Morning Call newspaper in Paterson, NJ wrote about the play, ***"Jackie Robinson, as if to show Martin how a steal of home is accomplished by an artist, pilfered the bag in the top of the eighth. This time there was no question about Robby being safe."***

Catcher Yogi Berra saw it differently. Drebinger wrote, ***"Berra almost jumped out of his shoes as he protested vigorously to Umpire Summers."***

It was the 18th time in Jackie Robinson's career he had stolen home. And it brought the Dodgers to within a run at 6 - 5.

You can watch this exciting play on YouTube by typing into the search, "Jackie Robinson Steals Home."

On the video it appears that Berra was in position to tag Robinson, but Jackie got his toe onto the plate before Berra could get his glove down.

It was an electrifying play. A daring dash by one of the Dodgers' oldest players. And it enthralled the sportswriters as well as the fans. Don Murray of the Bridgewater, NJ Courier News wrote, ***"If you had to pick out a single play in the game that stands above all others, it would be tough to pass up Robinson's feat - no pun intended. One of the best baserunners ever to come down the pike, Robinson hasn't been doing much base stealing the past few years because his once-speedy legs have gone too many miles. But as he headed home on Whitey Ford's windup in the eighth yesterday Jackie was flying like a rookie on a rampage."***

When Whitey finally got to pitch again, Kellert knocked a single to center. And then Ford got the side retired when Jim Gilliam popped to Gil McDougald who safely corralled this ball for the 3rd out.

Yankees 6 Dodgers 5 - middle of the 8th inning

The Dodgers' 3rd pitcher of the game was Clem Labine. He was perhaps the most reliable relief pitcher in the Dodgers' bullpen. He appeared in a league high 60 games in 1955. He even started 8 games during the season as needed. And he had a record of 13 - 5. The 29 year old had been on the Dodgers' staff since 1951. He had little trouble with the Yankees, not allowing a runner past 1st base.

So now the Dodgers had one more chance to tie the game in the top of the 9th and had their 2, 3 and 4 batters due up.

Casey Stengel decided to bring in relief pitcher Bob Grim. Ford had only allowed 3 earned runs but had given up 9 hits and 4 walks in 8 innings. Stengel felt more comfortable with a fresh righty pitcher for the 9th. And while Grim had only a so-so year in 1955, he had won 20 in 1954.

Grim got Pee Wee Reese looking for out number 1. Duke Snider hit a line shot past Collins at 1st base and into right field for a single, to put the tying run on base. Next up was the catcher, Roy Campanella. Campy had been one of the most fearsome hitters in baseball since his debut in 1949. He had won MVP awards in 1951 and 1953 and had just completed an MVP worthy season in 1955.

Drebinger wrote, ***"a right-handed hitter, finding himself at a disadvantage in a park that has acres of territory in left, tried desperately to stroke the ball for a homer into the right-field stand. But the effort fell a few feet short."***

Hank Bauer caught Campy's drive just in front of the wall in right field for the 2nd out. Just a few more feet and the Dodgers would have gone ahead 7 - 6. Instead Roy Campanella had gone 0 for 5 on the day and the Dodgers were down to their last hope.

Carl Furillo, came to the plate as that last hope. And Brooklyn fans had strong reason to believe. Furillo was 3 for 3 and had walked, reaching base in all 4 plate appearances against Ford.

But Bob Grim stuck him out.

And game 1 was in the books.

Yankees 6 Dodgers 5 - FINAL SCORE

Post-Game Analysis

This morning, Jimmy Powers of the New York Daily News summed up the game in his Powerhouse column:

"(1) Newcombe was miserable. Lacked competitive spark; (2) Campy was 0 for 5"

Those two items are certainly large factors in what cost the Dodgers the game. Two of their stars, the ace pitcher and the soon to be 3-time MVP had poor games.

But the Dodgers are "unshaken" by the loss according to Pee Wee Reese who authored an article in today's Yonkers Herald Statesman. Reese wrote, ***"There was no depression in the clubhouse after the game... Nobody is down and we all feel we are going to win the Series.***

Then focusing on the positive, Reese wrote about Jackie Robinson, ***"I felt like Robby was going to break loose. Never was there a better steal of home than he pulled in the eighth and the Yankees will have a lot more trouble with him before the series ends."***

Walter Alston expressed similar sentiments to Reese in his post-game interview with Roscoe McGowen of the New York Times, ***"You don't like to lose that first one of course. But none of the boys sound down-hearted about it. They're still confident and so am I."***

No one is counting the Dodgers out after just one game, but it certainly wasn't the start Brooklyn was looking for as they try to win their 1st World Series. John Drebinger opened his front page article in the New York Times with this, ***"It may yet come to pass that the Dodgers will win their first world series. But they took one long stride in the wrong direction yesterday.***

The fact of the matter is that game 1 could have gone either way. And the World Series can still go to either club. There were many opportunities for the Dodgers to have come out on top. Roy Campanella told McGowen, ***"That one I got hold of in the ninth was really hit. Oh, if I had only hit it higher***

instead of on a line. It would have been in the right field stands, no doubt about it."

And if it did go in the stands the final score would have been Dodgers 7 – Yankees 6.

Neither team was able to seal or steal the World Series.

It was a close game and it portends to be a close series.

Joe Collins didn't seal the World Series advantage for the Yankees even though he had the biggest game of his life.

Jackie Robinson didn't steal game one for the Dodgers even though he stole home in electrifying fashion.

The Sports Time Traveler can't wait to experience game 2!

Chapter Twenty

1955 World Series Game 2 - The Third Out That Never Came

YANKEE STADIUM - Friday, September 30, 1955

Before yesterday afternoon's 2nd game of the 1955 World Series, Yankees' skipper Casey Stengel was concerned. He told Jim McCulley of the New York Daily News that even though his team had won the 1st game, he was worried about starting a lefty again.

The Dodgers' lineup is stacked with powerful right-handed batters. And the book on Brooklyn is that you can't pitch a lefty against them. Arthur Daley in the New York Times wrote yesterday morning, ***"The Brooks are supposed to devour left-handers whole."*** National League managers adhered to this thinking during the regular season. In 154 games, the Dodgers faced lefty starters just 11 times. And those teams often got bashed by Brooklyn's bats.

On May 29th, the Giants' Johnny Antonelli lasted just 1 and 2/3 innings giving up 4 runs. Antonelli went on to win 14 games during the season.

On June 16th, Joe Nuxhall of the Reds, who won 17 games in 1955, lasted only 4 innings, giving up 3 runs in a loss.

Lino Dinoso of the Pirates lasted just 2 innings and gave up 5 runs on July 3rd.

Don Liddle of the Giants lasted only 3 innings, giving up 4 runs on July 27th.

Luis Arroyo of the Cardinals only made it 1 inning on July 31st in a Dodgers rout.

It was ugly for most lefties against the 1955 Dodgers.

But a lefty hurler, 35-year-old Tommy Byrne, was Stengel's 2nd best starter in 1955. And we're back here in a time when the concept of "data analytics" doesn't exist, where managers make decisions based on experience and their gut. And Stengel had a feeling about Byrne. When Stengel has a feeling he goes with it. After all, he guided the Bronx Bombers to win 5 consecutive World Series titles from 1949 - 1953.

Stengel told McCulley, ***"I heard all about the Dodgers and left handers, how they murder them, but we were playing in a big park and the wind was blowing the right way."***

If Stengel had seen the analytics, he wouldn't have had too much to be worried about at all. In 1955, Tommy was Terrific pitching in the House That Ruth Built. He started 10 games and won 8 of them with an ERA of just 1.57. While on the road, he had an ERA of just under 5. In addition, and perhaps even more important, Byrne pitched just as well against righty batters as lefty batters in 1955.

So Tommy Byrne, whose career had been resurrected after he had been relegated to the Pacific Coast League in 1954, was going to get to start a World Series game for just the 2nd time, the 1st since he lasted only 3 and 1/3 innings against the Dodgers in game 4 of the 1949 World Series.

Walter Alston Confident

There was no outward concern from the Dodgers' manager Walter Alston. After the game 1 loss, he informed Roscoe McGowen of the New York Times, "(the players) ***are still confident and so am I."***

But inwardly he had to have some doubts. He was sending righty Billy Loes to the mound. Billy had made just 19 starts in 1955, as he battled shoulder issues all season. Loes has been in the starting rotation for Brooklyn since 1952. But he had only made 5 starts since the middle of July.

However, Alston didn't have a lot of choices. Alston's #2 starter, Carl Erskine, was dealing with a sore arm, and he was being held out in the hopes his arm might be ready for game 3 or 4 in Ebbets Field.

And his only other regular starter in 1955 was 23-year-old Johnny Podres. Two years ago in 1953, as a rookie, just 4 days past his 21st birthday, Podres had started the crucial game 5 of the 1953 World Series. He gave up a homer to the 1st batter of the game, and he couldn't get out of the 3rd inning in what turned into a Yankees' rout.

But who else could Walter Alston turn to?

NOTE from The Sports Time Traveler

I interrupt this chapter with a note from the present. In the classic book, "The Boys of Summer," **Roger Kahn noted that these beloved Dodger teams from the late Ebbets Field era had a nemesis that explained their inability to defeat the Yankees in World Series play,** *"they lacked the kind of pitching that makes victory sure."*

And this Brooklyn brain-teaser, about who to start in game 2, showcased Kahn's assertion. Walter Alston had to make a grave decision, and he simply didn't have any "sure" choices.

Alston could have made a bold move and started an interesting rookie on his bench. But he just wouldn't consider pitching Sandy Koufax. Koufax, only 19-years-old, was a bonus baby. Baseball rules required that he remain on the roster due to the size of his contract signing bonus. Yet Koufax had looked God like in a 2-hit 14 strikeout shutout on August 27th. It was one of the best pitched games in all of baseball in 1955. And in his very next start, a week later on September 3rd, Koufax threw a 5-hit shutout. At that point his ERA for the season over 30 innings was just 2.05, the best on the team by a wide margin. And his 2 shutouts tied him for the team lead for the entire season. Even the ace, Don Newcombe, only fired a single shutout in 1955.

But Alston was determined to only use Koufax in desperation according to syndicated columnist Harry Grayson. And Koufax had only looked so-so in his final 2 starts. So Alston apparently had no qualms about wasting Koufax's arm throwing extensive batting practice before game 1, which ensured no start or stint was coming for the teenager early in this World Series.

Of course, we know what Koufax was able to do in the next decade when he matured and figured out how to control his flame-throwing ability. And so it's easy to second guess a manager decades later.

But even one sportswriter of the time suggested Alston should give the ball to Koufax. John Fox of the Binghamton Press wrote on Sep 30, 1955, *"Brooklyn's best pitching bets were the inexperienced kids like Bessent, Spooner and Koufax."*

Now back to 1955.

So it was Billy Loes's job to stop the Yankees and even up the 1955 series. Loes didn't have stellar stats. His 3.59 ERA was higher than all the Yankees' top starters. What Loes did have was experience. He had started World Series games against the Yankees in 1952 and 1953. Both times he had pitched quality starts, yielding 3 earned runs in 8 innings.

But Loes had never pitched in Yankee Stadium.

Play Ball!

Tommy Byrne got the Dodgers 1-2-3 to open the game.

In the bottom of the 1st, Hank Bauer led off for the Yankees and singled. With a full count on the 2nd batter, Gil McDougald, Bauer took off for 2nd base. McDougald struck out and Roy Campanella gunned down Bauer at 2nd for a double play. Bauer pulled a muscle on the play.

Then Loes got Irv Noren to fly out to Duke Snider in center and the 1st inning was over.

Despite the pulled muscle, Hank Bauer took his spot in right field for the Yankees in the top of the 2nd.

Byrne got through the most fearsome part of the Dodgers' order in the 2nd, yielding just a walk to Carl Furillo.

In the bottom of the 2nd, Loes hit Yogi Berra leading off. Then he struck out Joe Collins, the man who had hit 2 home runs in game 1, and followed that by striking out Elston Howard, who had also hit a homer in the 1st game. Loes finished off the side by striking out Billy Martin as well. In 2 innings of work, Loes already had 4 strikeouts.

It looked like a pitching duel was on.

Dodgers 0 Yankees 0 - end of 2 innings

Before the start of inning 3, Hank Bauer had to come out of the game, as he was in severe pain from the muscle strain. Bob Cerv replaced Bauer in the outfield. Now the Yankees were down 2 outfielders as Mickey Mantle was out with a muscle tear and was feared lost for the entire series.

Byrne set the Dodgers down in order once more. And Loes faced just the minimum 3 batters as well. The game remained scoreless after 3.

In the top of the 4th, Pee Wee Reese led off with a line drive that went all the way to the wall in the right field corner. Reese wound up on 2nd with a double. Next up, Duke Snider drilled another line drive to the right field corner. Reese came racing home without a play at the plate, and for the 2nd day in a row, the Dodgers were the 1st team to score.

On the play, Snider thought a fan reached out and touched the ball, and assumed he had an automatic double. He slowed down as he got to 1st base. Snider then realized there was no call for the automatic double, but he tried to go for 2nd base anyway. Right fielder Elston Howard gathered the ball in the corner and threw out Snider at 2nd. Had Snider been running all the way, he would have had 2nd base.

The Dodgers all insisted that they saw the fan touch the ball. Dodgers' 1st base coach Jake Pitler pleaded with umpire Augie Donatelli to no avail. The Dodgers insisted that Donatelli was not in a position to see the play.

After the game, Howard, who was closer to the ball than anyone else on the field, told a UPI reporter that the ball, ***"hit the ground, bounced up against a wire gate, and hit the ground again."***

With the bases clear, Tommy Byrne walked Roy Campanella and got Carl Furillo to fly out. Then with 2 outs, Gil Hodges whacked a ball to deep left that produced an enormous roar from the crowd, but Yankees' Irv Noren was there to catch it. Byrne had held the heart of the Dodgers' order to 1 run in the 4th. But had Snider been safe at 2nd with no outs, things might have played out differently.

Dodgers 1 Yankees 0 - middle of the 4th

The bottom of the 4th inning started well for Billy Loes. After yielding a single to Gil McDougald, Irv Noren belted a grounder that Gil Hodges scooped up near 1st base. He stepped on the bag and threw to Reese at 2nd base. Reese put the tag on McDougald and the Dodgers had a double play. Two down.

Loes appeared on his way to putting another "0" on the scoreboard for the Yankees. With one more out, Loes could assure the Dodgers would still be ahead when the halfway mark of the game passed in the middle of the 5th.

Maybe Loes was already thinking ahead when he was facing Yogi Berra. Berra no doubt was thinking of retribution for being hit by Loes in the 2nd. Berra won the battle with Loes as he singled to left center.

Next up was the hero of game 1, Joe Collins. Perhaps Loes was leery of allowing Collins to hit his 3rd homer in 2 games. Loes threw 4 straight balls to issue his 1st walk of the game.

Now there were 2 outs and runners on 1st and 2nd.

Loes still needed 1 more out to retire the side.

Next up was Elston Howard, the man who had hit a home run in game 1 on his 1st ever World Series at bat. Howard had also been a Loes strikeout victim in the 2nd. This time he singled to left field. Berra hustled home, but he was aided by Jackie Robinson's unfortunate attempt to cut off Junior Gilliam's throw. Berra scored, and the Yankees had tied the game at 1.

Jack Hand of the AP wrote about the play, ***"As Berra scored the tying run there was great debate in the stands as to whether Gilliam's peg would have cut down the runner if Robinson hadn't interfered."***

Now there were still 2 outs and runners still on 1st and 2nd.

Loes still needed just 1 more out to be done with the Yankees in the 4th.

The feisty Billy Martin came to the plate. Martin was the man who took it upon himself to attempt a steal of home in game 1. Martin was also the man who despite batting just .257 back in 1953, went out and hit .500 in the World Series, amassing a record 12 hits. Martin promptly hit a sharp grounder into left field, keeping Junior Gilliam busier than he wished. That scored another run and gave the Yanks the lead at 2 - 1.

This brought Walter Alston out of the dugout for a conversation with Loes. Despite having put 4 consecutive batters on base with 2 outs, Alston decided to let Loes stay in the game and try to get out of the inning.

It was an interesting decision, perhaps influenced by the fact that Loes spot in the batting order was coming up in the top of the 5th. Alston may have figured he would be taking Loes out for a pinch hitter anyway, so why not leave him in to get the last out instead of wasting another pitcher who he also would pinch hit for in the 5th.

With Loes staying in the game, Yankees' manager Stengel made a move. He took light hitting righty shortstop Phil Rizzuto out, bringing in a left-handed pinch hitter, Eddie Robinson, to bat against the righty Loes.

Loes still needed just 1 more out to end the 4th inning.

Loes perhaps rattled by the pressure at this point, hit Robinson in the middle of the back on the 1st pitch.

And thus, Billy Loes entered the record books for the dubious distinction of being the 1st pitcher ever to hit 2 batters in a single World Series game.

Now there were 2 outs and the bases loaded and Billy Loes still needed just one more out.

Next to the plate was the Yankees' pitcher Tommy Byrne. Early in his career, Byrne was a fine hitting pitcher. In 1948, he had batted .326 in 46 at bats. And he batted over .270 across 1950 and 1951. He got a hit in his only at bat in the 1949 World Series.

Then in 1954, playing for Seattle in the Pacific Coast League for most of the year, Byrne saw frequent action as a pinch hitter. In 176 at bats he hit 7 homers, drove in 39 runs and batted .295. Extrapolated over a full season that would have been a 20+ homer / 100+ RBI year. When the Yankees brought him back up to the big leagues at the end of 1954, Byrne went 7 for 19 from the plate for a .368 average. What's more is that 5 of those 7 hits were for extra bases.

The bottom line is that Tommy Byrne could hit.

And so it was no surprise that with the bases loaded, Casey Stengel chose to let Byrne stay in the game to hit.

Loes 1st pitch was a ball. His 2nd pitch was smashed by Byrne. It was a line drive that whizzed right by Loes's ear according to Jack Hand. It went into center field for a single and drove in Howard and Martin.

Tommy Byrne had just broken open the game as the Yankees now led 4 - 1.

Now Walter Alston took out Billy Loes, the pitcher who couldn't get the 3rd out.

For the 2nd game in a row, Alston gave the ball to Don Bessent, and Bessent promptly got the 3rd out that Billy Loes could not.

It had been a catastrophe for Billy Loes. 6 consecutive batters had reached base, all with 2 outs, and the Dodgers were now in a 3 run hole.

Yankees 4 Dodgers 1 - end of 4 innings

The Dodgers got 1 run back in the top of the 5th when Jackie Robinson walked and scored after Don Zimmer and Junior Gilliam singled.

In the bottom of the 5th, Alston brought in Karl Spooner to pitch, replacing Bessent who had been removed for a pinch hitter. Spooner was making his first World Series appearance. He had been an interesting pitcher for the Dodgers. Brought up at the close of the 1954 season for the first time, Spooner had thrown 2 spectacular shutouts in 4 days, throwing 15 strikeouts in the 1st shutout and another dozen in the 2nd. Spooner became the 1st pitcher ever to throw 15 strikeouts in their first game.

This fueled great anticipation for Spooner heading into the 1955 season. But a spring training injury delayed his season debut until mid-May. This season, in 1955, Spooner pitched in 29 games, starting 14, with moderate success as he sported an 8 - 6 record and a 3.65 ERA.

Somehow Spooner reverted back to his end of 1954 form, as he shut down the Yankees in the 5th, 6th and 7th giving up no hits and striking out 5. And when Spooner came out for a pinch hitter, Clem Labine continued the hitless streak in the 8th inning.

But Tommy Byrne was nearly as good, allowing no hits in the 6th and 7th innings. In the 8th inning, with 2 outs, Byrne gave up his 1st hit since the 5th, issuing a single to Reese. Next up was the dangerous Duke. Snider had hit a mammoth upper deck home run in game 1. And he had driven in the Dodgers' 1st run in the 4th.

Now Tommy Byrne demonstrated a little baseball gamesmanship, according to syndicated columnist Jimmy Cannon (and other reporters). With the count full, Byrne yelled out to Duke, ***"We'll try a fastball."*** Cannon wrote, ***"The***

perfidious Byrne reared back, as they say in baseball circles, and fired - not a fast ball but a slider which broke seven inches... Mr. Snider missed it by six and a quarter." Byrne had struck out Snider to end another Dodgers threat.

After yielding 2 runs across the 4th and 5th, Byrne had been brilliant in the 6th - 8th innings. Jim Ogle of the Newark Star-Ledger wrote, ***"Byrne kept rolling along mixing up a curve, fastball and slider to the utter consternation of the Dodgers who are supposed to 'eat' lefthanders, but found Byrne indigestible. Tommy had a couple of perilous spots but kept throwing as if it were batting practice."***

Byrne was also aided by some sensational fielding. In the 7th inning, Berra nailed Gil Hodges, trying to steal 2nd, when Don Zimmer struck out. In the 8th, the Yankees got the first 2 outs by turning a more traditional double play from 2nd baseman Billy Martin to shortstop Jerry Coleman to 1st baseman Joe Collins.

As a result, the Yankees remained in the lead after 8 innings.

Yankees 4 Dodgers 2 - end of 8 innings

Now Brooklyn was down to their last at-bats. But the Dodgers had their 3 righty power men coming to the plate against the lefty Byrne. Roy Campanella led off with a high pop-up. Campy was now 0 for 8 in the series. Next up, Carl Furillo flied out to left. The last batter, Gil Hodges, struck out.

Tommy Byrne was the winner of game 2 of the 1955 World Series. He did what everyone said couldn't be done. He pitched a complete game victory over the Brooklyn Dodgers. He became the only lefty to perform this feat in 1955. And in doing so, he gave the Yankees a commanding 2 games to none lead over the Dodgers.

Byrne had also capped off one of the most unlikely of comebacks at 35 years of age. He had been an all-star starter for the Yanks back in 1950. But he looked finished as a big leaguer in 1951, when his ERA ballooned to 6.86 and the Yankees dealt him to the lowly Browns. From there things had gotten worse. In 6 starts for the White Sox in 1953, his ERA was over 10! And then the Senators gave him a try, and he went 0 - 5.

In 1954, Byrne was out of the majors. But he gave baseball one more try with the Seattle Rainiers of the Pacific Coast League. He won 20 games in 30 starts. He pitched so well that the Yankees brought him back. This year, in 1955, he finished the season with the best winning percentage in the American League with a 16 - 5 record. And now Tommy Byrne had pitched a 5-hit gem in the World Series.

What a game it was for Tommy Byrne. A masterful complete game on the mound and the key hit of the game as well. For it was Byrne's 2-run single that broke open the game, making the score 4 - 1, and knocking out Dodgers' starter Billy Loes.

What's more, Byrne broke Brooklyn's spirit. John Craig of the Newark Star-Ledger wrote, ***"It was a far cry from the Dodger dressing room of Wednesday, when the Brooks were a raucous group. Today, they talked to reporters quietly, had nothing but praise for their conquerors and then dressed quickly and departed."***

And reporters in every paper are making sure today that the Dodgers and their fans know that no team has ever lost the first 2 games of a 7-game World Series and come back to win the title. Joe Trimble of the New York Daily News made sure to cite that statistic in the opening paragraph of his story today.

The 3rd Out That Never Came

From the Dodgers point of view, the story of the game was the 3rd out that never came. Billy Loes had 2 men down in the 4th and was leading 1 - 0, when he just couldn't retire the side. 6 consecutive batters reached base, resulting in 4 Yankees' runs, and that was the ballgame.

Sandy Koufax is Billy Loes's roommate on road trips, and Koufax had this to say in the New York Times, ***"His fast ball and his curve both were humming.***

I don't know what happened to him, but he quit throwing curves after the first three innings."

The Series Moves to Brooklyn

Now the series will shift from the cavernous House that Ruth Built, Yankee Stadium, the cathedral of ballparks, to the Dodgers' beloved little band-box, Ebbets Field that can fit only about half the fans of its American League rival.

Dodgers' management is dismayed with the tiny seating capacity and perpetual parking problem that plagues Ebbets Field. In this morning's newspapers a UP article indicated the Dodgers have asked the celebrated architect and futurist, Buckminster Fuller, to study a new all-weather domed stadium for the Dodgers. Fuller is presently a visiting lecturer at Princeton University and he will conduct the study assisted by 25 graduate students.

In the meantime, The Sports Time Traveler will take the subway virtually to Brooklyn for game 3 of the 1955 World Series. I can't wait!

Chapter Twenty-One

1955 World Series Game 3 - Surprise! Surprise!

EBBETS FIELD, BROOKLYN - October 1, 1955

The Sports Time Traveler is in a constant state of amazement as I experience the 1955 World Series.

There was one surprise after another yesterday as the Fall Classic shifted from cavernous Yankee Stadium, where the Bronx Bombers captured the opening 2 games, to Ebbets Field, Brooklyn's little "band box" ballpark, for game 3, and a must win situation for the Dodgers.

No Surprise - Don't Drive to Ebbets Field

Yesterday morning the New York Times advised readers with tickets to NOT drive to Ebbets Field. They warned, ***"approaches to the home of the Dodgers are likely to be congested and parking accommodations are limited."*** The Subway was recommended as the way to go.

This is not much of a surprise as the problem of reaching Ebbets Field by car has been an issue in recent years as many fans moved out to the suburbs.

A Dome for the Dodgers?

What was a little surprise was the page 1 discussion of a new domed stadium.

Issues with Ebbets Field have been a much discussed topic here in 1955, and this morning, the AP ran a story with more details about the project underway by famed architect Buckminster Fuller to design a new domed stadium. The stadium will be 30 stories tall and have a diameter of 750 feet, twice as wide as any other domed building ever constructed. The story also made page 1 of the New York Times.

That the Dodgers need a new ballpark is no surprise. That it might be a grandiose domed stadium, the largest one ever, was a bit of a surprise.

The Mick is Back!

The first truly big surprise of the day came 10 minutes before the opening pitch when Yankees' manager Casey Stengel made a change to his lineup. He inserted the name Mickey Mantle batting 4th and playing center field. Mantle, just minutes earlier, had come to Casey and asked to play, according to radio announcer Bob Neal.

Mantle has blossomed into a true superstar here in 1955. He led the American League in home runs (37), triples (11) and walks (113). Mantle was the heart of the team, the heir apparent to Ruth, Gehrig and DiMaggio.

But Mickey had torn a muscle in the final week of the season and missed the first 2 games of the series. Without Mantle, the Yankees still managed to win both games. Now with Mantle back, the potential for a sweep had to be crossing the minds of all baseball fans.

Podres to Start

Walter Alston earlier had provided a smaller surprise when he announced that Johnny Podres would start game 3. Alston explained why his #2 starter Carl Erskine was not ready, ***"He is not yet 100%, so I know I can get only one game out of him."*** Alston's strategy is to save Erskine for that one game later in the series. It's a real gamble, since if the Dodgers lose this game, they'd be effectively done, down 3 games to none.

Erskine had been the Dodgers' #1 starter from 1952 - 1954 and started 29 games this year. Erskine also has the most World Series experience on the staff. He had beaten the Yankees in the 1952 World Series. The next year, he set the World Series record of 14 strikeouts in defeating the Yankees in game 3 of the 1953 World Series. Erskine had a record of 2 - 1 against the Yankees across the 1952 and 1953 World Series. The rest of the Dodgers staff were a combined 3 - 7. But Erskine's sore arm just wasn't ready.

So the ball was being given to the birthday boy, young Johnny Podres, who turned 23-years-old yesterday. He has been in the Dodgers' rotation since he was a 20-year-old rookie in 1953. Although his career ERA is over 4, he's shown flashes of brilliance. He threw back-to-back shutouts and had a record of 7 - 3 in mid-June. But he developed a sore arm and didn't complete a single game in 12 starts over the 2nd half of the season. And in his only World Series appearance in 1953, he lasted just 2 and 2/3 innings in a Dodgers' loss.

Desperate Dodgers fans must have been directing their prayers to the palm of Podres.

Yankees Turn to Turley

The Yankees' starter for game 3 was no surprise. Bullet Bob Turley was an all-star in 1955, and started more games than any other Yankees' hurler. He won 17 games, 6 of them in shutouts. The only issue with Turley's tossing was his control. He led the league in walks issued with 177.

Dodgers' Lineup Changes

In another minor surprise, Dodgers' manager Walter Alston, moved Junior Gilliam from left field to 2nd base and gave a start to Sandy Amoros in left. Don Zimmer, who had played 2nd base in the opening 2 games went to the bench. The purpose of the move was not to demote Zimmer, who had gone 2 for 5 with 2 RBIs in the opening games. Rather the idea was simply to get another lefty bat in the game to face the Yankees' right handed pitcher Turley.

The First Pitch

When it came time for the ceremonial 1st pitch, Tex Richards, the public address announcer, boomed out to the Brooklyn crowd, ***"Borough President John Cashmore will throw out the ball."*** In yet another surprise, laughter could be heard throughout the stands when the ball was not given to Cashmore but rather was thrown by New York Governor Averill Harriman. John Drebinger wrote in the New York Times, ***"Such slips in protocol are always taken in stride in Flatbush."***

Batter Up!

Game time temperature was a comfortable 70 degrees, but ***"the sky was gloomy,"*** according to Dick Young of the Daily News. It must have seemed like a bad omen for Brooklyn.

But the game started well for "dem Bums," as Johnny Podres cruised through the top of the 1st 1-2-3. He did get help from Carl Furillo, the master of right field in Ebbets, as he made a fine shoestring catch on the 3rd out to rob Yogi Berra of a hit.

In the bottom of the 1st, Turley got Jim Gilliam to fly out, but then walked Pee Wee Reese. With 1 out, he faced the Duke and struck him out. Then with 2 outs, Roy Campanella, hitless in 8 at bats in the series stepped to the plate.

Campanella got some wood on the 1st pitch, fouling if off. On the 2nd pitch, he got a lot more wood on the ball. He crushed it on a line drive into the lower deck in left center field. It was a 2-run homer, Campy's 1st hit of the series. And it gave the Dodgers the early lead for the 3rd consecutive game.

Next up was Carl Furillo. He sent a looping ball into right center. Mantle, running with only one good leg, made a ***"last lunging limp,"*** according to Dana Mozley in the Daily News, and caught the ball to end the inning.

Dodgers 2 Yankees 0 - end of 1st inning

In the top of the 2nd, Mickey Mantle led off. He drilled a Podres pitch over the 393 feet mark in center field for a homer in his 1st at bat of the series. Jack Hand of the AP noted that both Campanella and Mantle's homers would have been catchable fly balls in the vast left and center field spaces inside Yankee Stadium.

Next up, Bill Skowron, playing 1st base instead of Joe Collins to get another righty bat in the lineup, hit a double to left field. And suddenly Podres was looking shaky.

After Podres got Elston Howard to ground out and Billy Martin on strikes, Walter Alston came to the mound to discuss whether Podres should pitch to Phil Rizzuto, or give him a pass and try to get the 3rd out with the pitcher Turley up next. The decision was to pitch to Rizzuto, and he singled to left. Sandy Amoros fired the ball to Campanella to catch Skowron going for home. The throw was there in plenty of time, Skowron didn't even slide, he just ran straight towards Campy. According to Dick Young in the Daily News, ***"Campanella stepped aside and tried to pick him off with a stiff, two-arm swipe."*** But as Campy made contact with Skowron the ball, ***"flew out of his bare hand,"*** according to Drebinger. Skowron scored and the game was tied.

While the focus was on trying to catch Skowron at home, Phil Rizzuto was scooting around the bases. And when the ball got away from Campanella, Rizzuto charged for home. The ball ***"trickled toward the lip of the*** (Brooklyn) ***dugout,*** according to Young, and then it ***"settled into a little blind nook behind the bat-rack."*** Had the ball not dropped into the nook, it would have been a live ball, and Rizzuto's run would have counted. But the umpires invoked the ground rules and sent Rizzuto back to 3rd base.

Podres finally got out of the inning when the pitcher Turley grounded out.

Mantle on the Move

Now with the Yankees going into the field, Stengel moved Mantle to right, hoping to minimize any running Mickey would have to do in the outfield. Elston Howard moved to left field and Bob Cerv took over in center.

The move paid off right away, as Gil Hodges hit a fly to center that Cerv caught. The 2nd batter, Jackie Robinson singled to center field, keeping Cerv busy. Then Sandy Amoros, in his 1st World Series plate appearance was hit by Turley. Next, Johnny Podres, a .250 lifetime hitter, tried to bunt the runners over. The bunt was perfect. Turley was slow getting off the mound and fumbled the ball according to Lud Duroska of the Newark Star-Ledger. Turley couldn't make a play. Everyone was safe and the bases were loaded with Dodgers with just 1 out.

The Jackie Robinson Show

Now that Jackie was on 3rd base, he teased that he was going to dash for home as he had done successfully in game 1. Dick Young wrote, ***"As Turley pitched to Gilliam, Robinson's little feints became big ones. With each pitch, Jackie would take a dry run almost halfway down the line. Turley with one eye on Robinson, one on the plate, only got one strike over to Gilliam."***

With the count at 3 balls and 1 strike to Junior Gilliam, you can see how Jackie Robinson must have had the 25-year-old Turley totally unnerved. On YouTube type in the search bar, "1955 World Series Game 3: Yankees @ Dodgers." At 2:45 on the tape, watch how Robinson is more than one-third of the way down the line as Turley pitches. It's ball 4, and Robinson can now walk home. The run put the Dodgers back ahead 3 - 2, and there is no doubt that Jackie Robinson manufactured this one.

Shower Time for Turley

That was it for Bob Turley. Casey came to the mound and called for Tom Morgan. Morgan had been a reliable reliever for Stengel in 1955, winning 7 and saving 11 games with a 3.25 ERA. And unlike Turley, Morgan didn't walk many batters, only 24 walks issued in 72 innings in 1955. But Morgan promptly walked Pee Wee Reese putting the Dodgers ahead by 2 runs.

It could have been a very big inning with Snider and Campy coming up, but Morgan settled down and got Snider to hit a grounder to 1st. Skowron threw to Berra at home for the force out. Then Campy hit a liner to Billy Martin at 2nd to end the inning.

Dodgers 4 Yankees 2 - end of 2 innings

Back on the mound after a long time standing on the bases, Johnny Podres breezed through the top of the Yankees' lineup 1-2-3 for the 2nd time in the game.

And after a leadoff double to Carl Furillo, Morgan shut down the bottom of the Dodgers' lineup to end the 3rd inning.

In the top of the 4th, Podres again sent down the Yankees in order when he got Mantle to ground out and then struck out Skowron and Howard.

In the bottom of the 4th inning, the Dodgers had the top of the order up, and they proved too much for Morgan. A single by Gilliam, a walk by Snider and another single by Campanella led to a run. Then Carl Furillo lofted a high fly ball down the left field line. Elston Howard tracked the ball as it went into foul territory. He could have let it drop, but he decided to make the catch for the 2nd out, and this allowed Duke Snider to easily tag up and score from 3rd base.

The Dodgers had now opened up a 4 run lead at 6 - 2.

In the top of the 5th, Podres issued a walk and nothing else. He got Bob Cerv to strikeout for the 2nd time to retire the side. Podres had not allowed a hit since the 2nd inning.

In the bottom of the 5th, the Yankees sent a new pitcher to the mound, Johnny Kucks. A 23-year-old rookie, Kucks had been a steady pitcher for Stengel, starting in 13 games and relieving in 16 others during the year with an acceptable ERA of 3.41. Kucks kept the Dodgers quiet in the 5th.

As the 6th inning got underway, Podres gave up his first base hit since the 2nd when Gil McDougald singled to center. Berra followed that up with another single to center, and suddenly the Yankees had 2 on and no outs and the makings of a comeback inning with Mickey Mantle stepping up to the plate.

Walter Alston made his 2nd trip to the mound now, and he had Don Bessent up in the bullpen. But Alston left Podres in the game. Podres served Mantle a steady diet of curve balls. And Mantle went after one and grounded to Reese at shortstop. With Mantle unable to run well, this was a perfect double play ball. Now there were 2 outs, and Gil McDougald was on 3rd. In a moment, Podres got out of the inning when Skowron bounced one to short.

Kucks did a fine job handling the heart of the Dodgers' order in the bottom of the 6th and the score remained 6 - 2 Dodgers after 6 innings.

In the top of the 7th, Podres got 2 quick outs and then walked Phil Rizzuto for the 2nd time. Rizzuto was now the only player in the game to reach base each time he came to the plate. The next batter, Andy Carey, pinch-hitting for Kucks, drilled a ball that bounced off the wall in the left field corner for a triple. Rizzuto scored to make it a 6 - 3 game. Podres got out of the inning when he got Cerv to strikeout for the 3rd consecutive time.

In the bottom of the 7th, Stengel sent another rookie to the mound. 25-year-old Tom Sturdivant had pitched in 33 games with a solid 3.16 ERA. The

1st batter he faced was Hodges, who rapped a long drive to left field. Rookie Elston Howard ***"made a fine leaping catch of Gil Hodges's fly off the left field wall,"*** according to Drebinger.

The 2nd batter he faced was Jackie Robinson. Robinson shot a hot liner down the 3rd base line that went all the way to the wall in left, where Elston Howard retrieved it.

The Jackie Robinson Show - Episode 2

Now another Jackie Robinson show began. Dick Young wrote, ***"He suckered*** (Elston) ***Howard. Jackie took a wide turn of second as Howard ran down the ricocheting ball. The Yankee rookie made the mistake of throwing behind Robby, believing he could cut him off. That's all Robinson needed. As the ball went to second, Robby went to third, sliding in under Martin's hurried high relay."***

When Sandy Amoros singled to right field, Robinson jogged home with the Dodgers' 7th run, and Jackie Robinson received a loud cheer. Once again, a run had scored because of Jackie's base-running smarts.

Drebinger marveled about Robinson outwitting the Yankees, ***"At 36, Jackie still is one of the greatest base runners the majors have seen."***

The Dodgers weren't done. After Podres bunted Amoros to 2nd and Gilliam walked, Pee Wee Reese singled to center and the Dodgers scored their 8th run.

Dodgers 8 Yankees 3 - end of 7 innings

Podres got his 3rd 1-2-3 inning in the 8th when all 3 Yankees grounded out.

Sturdivant gave up a double to Campy in the bottom of the 8th, but nothing else.

In the top of the 9th, Podres gave up an opening single to Skowron, but Podres followed that up with 3 straight pop-ups, and the game was in the books.

A Surprise Hero

The Brooklyn Dodgers had won convincingly 8 - 3, and Johnny Podres, the 23-year-old birthday boy was the hero of the game. He had pitched a complete game, his first one since June! He had needed just 107 pitches to stop the Yankees. Of his 107 pitches, 77 were strikes. It was the best birthday gift he ever had.

It was a great victory for the Dodgers. Never before had they won a World Series game by 4 or more runs. And more important they were back in the series with a chance to tie the next day.

After the game, Roscoe McGowen in the New York Times reported that Podres, ***"had a crowd eight men deep in front of his locker. Everybody wanted to talk to the young left-hander..."***

Podres told Charley Feeney of the Newark Star Ledger, ***"It's just wonderful, just wonderful. I felt great out there... I was going so good I was bubbling over with confidence."***

Podres told McGowen, ***"A good pitcher can beat anybody and I had good stuff today. That's all there is to it."***

He told Jim McCulley of the Daily New, ***"I never had a better assortment of stuff."***

And Podres told Jack Lang of the Staten Island Advance, ***"My changeup was the best I've ever had. I threw it about 25 or 30 times. And I paced myself better in this game than I ever had before."***

About Mantle's homer Podres said, ***"That one was a bad pitch. I wanted to throw it outside but I got it over the plate. I think just above his knees and he smacked it good didn't he?"***

Catcher Roy Campanella told Charley Feeney, ***"When I saw that change-up in the first inning, I knew we had something."*** Feeney wrote that Campanella told him, ***"Podres beat the Yankees on the strength of the 'best change-up he's had all year.'"***

Pee Wee Reese told McCulley, ***"It was one of the finest pitching performances I've seen anywhere... Speed alone won't beat the Yankees, you have to give them soft stuff and mix it up, and Podres sure mixed 'em up. He had them off stride all the time."***

A Surprise Encore Performance

Dick Young also credited Jackie Robinson as providing the key to the Dodgers triumph, ***"Robinson was magnificent. He was the spark the discouraged Brooks needed. For these two hours, and a little more, he was young again. His cap covered his gray hairs and his spirit disguised the age in his legs. On the bases, he taunted the pitchers till they hated him the way they used to... He suckered outfielder Elston Howard into an extra base. He smacked a single and a double. He handled seven grounders, some of them toughies, in a busy day at third base. And all the while, he kept chattering encouragement to the kid on the mound."***

No one should underestimate the value that Robinson provided by constantly talking to Podres on the mound. Jackie told McCulley, ***"I just kept talking to him because I wanted to keep him alert. I didn't want him to let up for a single minute, and he didn't. What I liked about him today was his heart. We just had to win this one."***

The Dodgers Got What They Needed

This morning, the Staten Island Advance published an article by Pee Wee Reese in which he described what the win did for the club, ***"There's real confidence in our gang. You never heard more of the old-time pepper than there was on the field yesterday, and we have that feeling we'll win. We've got what we need."***

The Biggest Surprise of All

Last night, long after the game, Johnny Podres got the biggest surprise of the day. He was invited to a family friend's house in Staten Island, Dr. and Mrs. J.W. Wisnefski at 594 Jewett Avenue. And there they had a surprise birthday party for Johnny Podres - the man who pitched the Dodgers back into the 1955 World Series.

The Sports Time Traveler can't wait for game 4 at Ebbets Field this afternoon.

Chapter Twenty-Two

1955 World Series Game 4 - Campy, Hodges and the Duke

EBBETS FIELD, BROOKLYN - October 2, 1955

Walter Alston's Peaceful Mind

After game 3 concluded, Dodgers' manager Walter Alston had to feel much better than he did the previous morning when the Dodgers were down 2 games to none. Because in game 3, Alston's most doubtful starter, young Johnny Podres, who didn't even have a winning record in 1955, threw masterfully and brought Brooklyn back into the series with an 8 - 3 victory.

And before game 4 yesterday, Alston had to take comfort in knowing that even though the Dodgers were still down 2 games to 1, they had 2 more games at Ebbets Field. Even better, he could now go to his 2nd best starter to pitch game 4. It was a man he held out earlier in the series to give his sore arm more rest. He would be sending to the mound the ace of the staff from 1952 to 1954, a 28-year-old player in his prime, who had pitched in 7 World Series games against the Yankees going back to 1949, and in his last World Series appearance, in 1953, had set the record of 14 strikeouts in a single game. Alston was going to hand the ball to a Dodger who had been one of the Boys of Summer since the band was fully assembled in 1948 - Carl Erskine.

Casey Stengel's Uncertainty

Yesterday morning Casey Stengel couldn't have been very confident about his game 4 starter. After his big 3 starters, who all pitched in games 1 - 3, he didn't have a clear 4th starter for a game of this magnitude. There was no one left on the staff who had started more than 13 games in the 1955 season.

The leading candidate was Don Larsen. The 25-year-old had only become a part of the rotation in the final 2 months of the season. And many newspaper reports after game 3 indicated Larsen had been named as the game 4 starter.

Larsen was in just his 1st season as a Yankee after being acquired in a whopping 17-player trade with the Baltimore Orioles following the 1954 season.

Not only did Larsen have no World Series experience, but last year, in 1954, he had the dubious distinction of recording the worst winning percentage of any pitcher in major league baseball since 1916. Pitching for the Orioles, who lost 100 games, Larsen had a record of 3 - 21.

This year, Larsen had a sore shoulder early in the season, so he was sent to down to AAA in Denver, where he went 9 - 1.

He was brought back up the Yankees at the end of July and threw a 4 hitter on July 31st. He became a part of the rotation and had a record of 8 - 1 after coming up back up from Denver. Overall, in professional baseball in 1955 Larsen was 18 - 3. Quite an improvement from 1954! This is the largest winning percentage improvement in baseball history.

The Alternatives

Casey had 2 other pitchers on the staff who had started 10 or more games.

23-year-old rookie, Johnny Kucks, had shown some strong promise early in the season. He threw a shutout on July 24th, and had been in the rotation most of June and July. But then he was taken out of the rotation when Larsen arrived. Kucks had not started a game since July 31st. There was some reason to believe in Kucks though, because in 23 innings of relief appearances since the beginning of August, Kucks had given up just 6 earned runs. But Kucks had pitched 2 innings in relief in game 3, so he was not a candidate to start game 4.

The only other option to start game 4 was Bob Grim. The 25-year-old Grim had been sensational as a rookie in 1954, winning 20 games while losing just 6. But Grim had the sophomore jinx in 1955. He got off to a horrific start to the season. His ERA climbed 6.06 in mid-May. Casey stuck with him in the rotation until mid-June, when he had a game in which he couldn't get more than 4 batters out before Casey had to retrieve the ball from him. After that, Grim never started a game the rest of the season, but did pitch 13 games in relief.

In his last 5 games in September, all in relief roles, Grim did not allow a single earned run in 15 innings, and only allowed 7 hits. And Grim had pitched one scoreless inning to close out game 1 for Whitey Ford.

Perhaps Casey would consider Grim as the hot pitcher.

Ultimately, Casey Stengel decided to stick with Don Larsen as his starter for game 4.

Erskine Takes the Mound

Carl Erskine faced Irv Noren to open game 4 in front of a ***"roaring" crowd of 36,242,"*** per John Drebinger in the New York Times.

Noren was the 2nd to last batter Erskine faced in his 14 strikeout gem 2 years ago, when he defeated the Yankees in game 3 of the 1953 World Series. In that game, Erskine walked Noren before getting Joe Collins to hit a grounder back to him that he threw to Gil Hodges to put his historic pitching performance in the books.

This time on a 2 and 2 pitch, Erskine fired a low curve on the inside corner that fooled Noren, who swung and missed for strike 3. Carl Erskine was off to a good start.

The 2nd batter was Gil McDougald. McDougald had 3 singles in 12 at bats so far in the series. The first 3 pitches were all inside and the count ran to 3 - 0. Erskine came back with a strike to make it a 3 - 1 count. Dick Young in the Daily News called that a ***"take pitch,"*** as McDougald was taking all the way. According to Dick Young the next pitch was a take pitch too. He wrote, ***"The next was taken by a fan in the left-center seats."*** McDougald had put the Yankees in front early 1 - 0 with the 5th World Series home run of his career.

Erskine got right back to work. He struck out Mickey Mantle, fooling him on a change up pitch for the 3rd strike. And then he got Yogi Berra to fly out to Duke Snider in center field.

In the bottom of the 1st inning, Larsen, pitching in a World Series for the 1st time, retired the side in order.

In the top of the 2nd, Erskine walked the leadoff man, Joe Collins. Elston Howard bunted Collins over to 2nd. Collins moved to 3rd base on a Billy Martin ground out. Now Erskine faced the weak hitting shortstop Phil Rizzuto. The "Scooter" had 2 hits in his last 3 at bats, and he hit a liner into center field that just eluded the outstretched glove of his long time Dodgers counterpart, Pee Wee Reese. That scored Collins and Erskine and the Dodgers were now behind in the game 2 - 0. Don Larsen then batted and flied out to Snider for the 3rd out.

In the bottom of the 2nd, Larsen breezed through the Brooklyn batters again yielding just a single to Gil Hodges. Dick Young noted about Larsen, ***"His control was unusually good during the first two frames."***

Yankees 2 Dodgers 0 - end of 2 innings

Erskine finally had an easy inning in the 3rd retiring the side in order including a 2nd strikeout of Mickey Mantle.

In the bottom of the 3rd, the Dodgers only got one hit, but it was a double down the left field line by Junior Gilliam, and with the hit-and-run on, it was enough to score Sandy Amoros from 1st base. Amoros had walked to leadoff the frame.

The top of the 4th began with Berra drilling a single into center field and Erskine issuing a walk to Joe Collins on 4 pitches. Even though he had only given up 3 hits and 2 walks and had struck out 3, including Mantle twice, Walter Alston saw something he didn't like. Erskine's elbow has been sore for months. He came to the mound and called for Don Bessent to come in to pitch.

Bessent had been an unexpected bright spot for the Dodgers bullpen in 1955. A 24-year-old rookie from Jacksonville, FL, Bessent got called up to the Dodgers in mid-July. He had been having a so-so season in his 5th full year in the minors. Playing in just AA ball in St. Paul he was 8 - 5 as a starter with a 3.58 ERA. But in the big leagues something clicked for him. He went 8 - 1 with 3 saves in 24 appearances (including 2 starts) and sported the lowest ERA on the team at 2.70. He had pitched 1 and 2/3 innings in the first 2 games and didn't allow a hit. Now he was entering the game in a jam. Runners on 1st and 2nd and no outs.

The 1st batter Bessent faced was Elston Howard. He bunted, but Bessent was able to get the ball to Jackie Robinson at 3rd base who tagged out the lead runner Berra. Now Bessent still had runners on 1st and 2nd with 1 out and Billy Martin the batter.

The lead runner was now Joe Collins. Collins broke for 3rd base. This was nearly as much of a surprise as Billy Martin trying to steal home in game 1, since Collins had not stolen a base all season. Bessent must have been stunned because his pitch bounced before reaching the plate and Collins was easily safe at 3rd. Also stunned on the play was Elston Howard, who stood frozen at 1st base, when he could have swiped 2nd.

Now there were runners on 1st and 3rd and still 1 out. The infield came in to defend against a suicide squeeze. Dick Young wrote, ***"Martin sent a bloop***

single just beyond the reach of Gilliam." It was a ball the 2nd baseman would have surely had if the infielders had not been playing in. Collins scored.

There must have been a hush among the Flatbush fans, for the Dodgers were now trailing 3 - 1 in a game that if they lost would put them down 3 games to 1 in the series. And the Yankees have never lost a World Series when they had a team down 3 games to 1.

Bessent did get the side retired quickly after the Martin single, when he got Phil Rizzuto to hit into a double play from Robinson to Gilliam to Hodges.

Yankees 3 Dodgers 1 - middle of the 4th inning

In the bottom of the 4th, Larsen came back out to the mound, having only allowed 2 hits so far in the game. The 1st batter was Roy Campanella. Campy promptly parked a ball into the seats in the left field corner, his 2nd homer in 2 days, to cut the deficit to a single run.

Next up, Carl Furillo beat out an infield chop that had bounded over Larsen's head for a single.

With a runner on 1st and no outs, Gil Hodges stepped in against Don Larsen. Dick Young described the action, ***"Hodges drove a high, lazy fly that landed atop the scoreboard in right-center. Gil's third series homer*** (in his career) ***had surprising carry and demonstrated his power to the opposite field."*** It was a 2-run shot and it catapulted the Dodgers into the lead 4 - 3.

After being shelled twice, Larsen managed to gather himself and got Jackie Robinson and Sandy Amoros to ground out before striking out Bessent to end the inning.

In the top of the 5th, the Yankees came right back and loaded the bases with 2 outs on singles by Irv Noren and Mickey Mantle and a walk to Yogi Berra. That prompted Walter Alston to go to his bullpen for his #1 reliever, Clem Labine.

Clem Labine had been a mainstay in the Dodgers' bullpen since 1951, and had been with the Dodgers organization since he was a 17-year-old in 1944. For the past 3 seasons he has pitched over 100 innings. And this season he appeared in a

National League high 60 games, and threw 144 innings, more than all but 3 of the Dodgers' starters. Alston had faith in Clem Labine.

Labine faced Joe Collins and got him to hit a grounder to 2nd baseman Junior Gilliam who tossed it to Reese to force out Yogi Berra at 2nd base to retire the Yankees in the 5th.

In the bottom of the 5th, Gilliam led off with a walk and stole 2nd. With the count 2 balls and no strikes on Pee Wee Reese, Casey Stengel came to the mound and took Larsen out of the game for Johnny Kucks.

Kucks immediately made a rookie mistake. After working the count to 3 and 2, Reese hit the payoff pitch. It was a hot grounder towards the hole between 1st baseman Joe Collins and 2nd baseman Billy Martin. Kucks didn't move off the mound. Kucks didn't anticipate that Joe Collins might be able to snag the ball before it darted through into right field. But Collins made a sensational play and got to the ball. The problem then for Casey, and Collins, was that Kucks, was not covering 1st base as the pitcher should have. Everyone was safe, Reese was on 1st base, Gilliam was on 3rd and there were no outs.

And now Duke Snider came to the plate.

If Kucks had covered, there would have been 1 out and a man on 2nd base, and Casey Stengel said after the game, in that scenario he would have issued an intentional walk to Snider. But now with men on 1st and 3rd, Casey had no choice but to let Kucks pitch to the Duke.

Now Kucks made his second mistake. He told Louis Efrat in the New York Times, ***"I got Snider out yesterday with a sinker pitch."*** But Kucks memory was faulty. In Snider's only at bat in game 3, he had singled off Kucks.

Here in game 4, Kucks tried to throw the same pitch to Snider. The Duke smashed it. Drebinger described the scene, ***"The Flatbush fans went delirious as Snider hammered a terrific home run high over the right-field barrier. The ball landed on top of an automobile parking lot on the other side of Bedford Avenue."***

Dick Young reported that the ball ricocheted off several automobiles before coming to rest.

We'll never know how many cars it touched, but what's in the books is that the ball caused 3 Dodgers to touch home plate.

Duke Snider's 3-run shot had blown open the game with the Dodgers taking a 7 - 3 lead.

It was Duke Snider's 7th career World Series homer, putting him in 4th place on the all-time list which now looks like this:

15 Babe Ruth

10 Lou Gehrig

8 Joe DiMaggio

7 Duke Snider

There were still no outs and Roy Campanella came to the plate. He lifted a long slicing fly to right field. Mickey Mantle on one good leg tried to grab it one-handed on the run, but it bounced off his glove and Campy had a double.

Then somehow, Kucks got it together and put down the next 3 Dodgers in a row to get out of the inning. But the big damage had been done. The Dodgers had a 4 run lead.

Dodgers 7 Yankees 3 - end of 5 innings

But it was too early to start any celebration. The Yankees pounded Labine to start out the 6th inning. Elston Howard singled, and then Billy Martin belted a ball into deep center field. Snider had been playing the 165 pound 2nd baseman shallow, and apparently couldn't conceive that the ball had been struck as hard as it was. The Duke got a late jump on the ball. Dick Young wrote, ***"The ball flew over him, skipped off the cinder track, and then got past Duke again as it bounded off the center wall."***

The result was a double and a run batted in for Martin, as Howard was able to score from 1st base.

After Labine got Phil Rizzuto to pop up, pinch-hitter Eddie Robinson singled to right field scoring Martin, and suddenly the Yankees were back in the game, down by just 2 runs.

The fireworks weren't over. Next up, Irv Noren hit a blast to right center. Bill Lee of the Hartford Courant described the play, ***"This is where Snider came in with a defensive gem almost as decisive as his home run. The Duke made an electrifying running grasp of Irv Noren's bid for extra bases and then took McDougald's fly for the third out."***

Duke Snider had saved at least another run and got Labine out of this near disastrous inning.

Dodgers 7 Yankees 5 - middle of the 6th inning

Having pinch hit for Kucks in the top of the 6th, the Yankees brought in Rip Coleman to pitch in the bottom of the inning. Coleman, a 24-year-old rookie, had pitched in just 10 games since coming up from Denver in mid-August. And he'd given up 17 earned runs in 29 innings of work. Now he was pitching in the World Series for the 1st time. Coleman gave up a lead off single to Sandy Amoros, who made his way to 2nd. If not for Phil Rizzuto's diving stab of a Pee Wee Reese grounder, Amoros would have scored. Coleman survived the inning yielding 2 singles, but no runs.

In the top of the 7th, Labine got Mickey Mantle on a hard grounder back to the box, and then retired Berra on a fly out to Amoros in left and Collins on a grounder to Junior Gilliam at 2nd.

In the top bottom of the 7th, Coleman was back on the mound for the Yankees. This time, he didn't get as lucky. Campanella led off with single up the middle. Then Carl Furillo took Coleman deep. Dick Young wrote. ***"Furillo drove off the free suit sign at the base of the scoreboard in right center. Only fast fielding Noren held runners at first and third."***

Such are the confines of Ebbets Field and the rebounds off the right field wall that Carl Furillo's blast off the wall resulted in only a single.

The next batter, Gil Hodges, then singled past Coleman who couldn't stab the ball, and Campy scored from 3rd base with the Dodgers' 8th run of the game.

The Dodgers had now ripped Rip Coleman for 5 hits in one official inning of work, and that was enough for Casey who replaced him on the mound with Tom Morgan.

Why Casey didn't go with Morgan earlier is hard to fathom. Morgan has been a mainstay on the Yankees pitching staff since 1951. He had been a spot starter until this year, when he pitched almost exclusively out of the bullpen, making 39 relief appearances and throwing a solid 3.25 ERA.

The Bullpen Man Who Wasn't There

What's even harder to fathom is a decision that Casey and the Yankees' made back in August that brought Coleman up from Denver. To make room for Coleman, the Yankees had to send veteran relief pitcher Jim Konstanty to Richmond until the minor league season ended after the first week in September. Stengel at the time was looking for another starter and wanted to see if Coleman could be the man. Konstanty, the former National League MVP in 1950 when he magically led the Philadelphia Phillies' Whiz Kids team to a pennant, had pitched fantastic for most of 1955. At the time Konstanty was rented out to Richmond he had a team leading 2.02 ERA in 38 appearances. His ERA had been as low as 0.89 on July 4th. At the time of his banishment to Virginia in August, Stengel had told George Burton in the Jersey Journal, ***"I want Konstanty's services back."***

And back he got him after Richmond's season ended. Konstanty rejoined the Yankees in the 2nd week of September and gave up no runs in his final 4 appearances.

But perhaps no one in Yankees management realized that by optioning Konstanty to Richmond he became ineligible for the postseason. And thus the Yankees were without arguably the best bullpen man on the team in 1955.

Tom Morgan's Turn

Taking over in mid-inning, Tom Morgan got Jackie Robinson to fly out to short center field. Then Amoros grounded to Martin at 2nd base, and the pitcher, Clem Labine, also grounded out. But the Dodgers had scored a run earlier and the score was now 8 - 5 Dodgers after 7 innings.

In the top of the 8th, Labine had another hitless inning. But once again he was aided by a highlight reel catch by Duke Snider. You can see that catch on the 5-minute highlight video of game 4 on YouTube by typing in the search bar, "1955 World Series Game 4: Yankees @ Dodgers." The Snider catch is at the 4:40 mark on the tape.

The Yankees brought in their 5th pitcher of the game to face the Dodgers in the bottom of the 8th. Tom Sturdivant was yet another rookie pitcher. The 25-year-old had a solid season with a 3.16 ERA in 33 appearances. Studivant performed well giving up just a bunt single to the leadoff hitter Gilliam.

Now the Yankees came up for their last at bat. Labine who had entered the game in the 5th inning was still on the mound in what was turning into one of his longest relief appearances of the year.

Labine had to face the top of the order. First up was Irv Noren. He was 1 for 4 with a single off Bessent. Noren lined out to Gil Hodges at 1st base. The #2 batter was Gil McDougald. After his 1st inning homer, McDougald had not reached base again. And he didn't this time either as he flied out to Carl Furillo in right. The #3 batter was Mickey Mantle. Mantle was playing valiantly through a painful torn muscle. Mickey was also 1 for 4, having singled off Bessent in the 5th. This time he bounced a ball back to Labine who tossed the ball to Hodges to end the game. Ed Corrigan of the AP wrote, ***"This was three-quarters of Mickey Mantle who played right field for the Yanks... he was of no use to the team."***

The Yankees had not put up much fight at the end. Bill Lee of the Hartford Courant wrote, ***"The Yanks went down meekly in the ninth."***

And so home field cooking did the trick for the Dodgers. The big bats came alive with homers by Campy, Hodges and the Duke. The fielding was sometimes spectacular. And the pitching was just good enough. The Dodgers won the game 8 - 5, and tied the World Series at 2 games apiece.

It's now a best of three and The Sports Time Traveler can't wait for game 5 later at 2:05pm today (Sunday) back here at Ebbets Field. The series will then move from Brooklyn back to the Bronx for game 6 tomorrow (Monday) with a 1pm starting time at Yankee Stadium. And should there be a game 7, it will also be at Yankee Stadium starting at 1pm on Tuesday. There are no off days in this World Series here in 1955.

Chapter Twenty-Three

1955 World Series Game 5 - Oh My Darling, Clem Labine!

EBBETS FIELD, BROOKLYN - October 3, 1955

The big story prior to game 5 of the 1955 World Series was that the Yankees would again be without their superstar player, Mickey Mantle. Mantle's torn leg muscle must have been made worse as he tried to play in games 3 and 4 after sitting out the opening 2 games. Casey Stengel told Dana Mozley of the New York Daily News, ***"He told me he could not run."***

In spite of the injury, which was suffered over a week ago, Mantle managed to hit a homer in game 3 and a single in game 4. But he is a liability in the outfield, even with him being shifted to right field. Casey had to scratch him from the lineup. And there is concern that Mantle is done for the series.

With Mantle out, Casey Stengel moved Joe Collins from 1st base to right field, and gave 34-year-old Eddie Robinson his 1st opportunity to start in a World Series game since he was on the Indians in 1948.

Hank Bauer, the Yankees' 2nd leading home run hitter with 20 in 1955, also was not available due to a similar leg muscle injury to Mantle's that he had sustained in game 1.

On the Dodgers side, the big a story was that Walter Alston would be entrusting this crucial game, the last one to be played at Ebbets Field in the series, to a rookie who had never thrown a single pitch in the big leagues until 77 days ago. In fact, 25-year-old Roger Craig had never even seen Ebbets Field until 77 days ago. But comforting Walter Alston in his bold decision is that the rookie, Craig, actually had the best ERA of any starter on the Dodgers staff in 1955 at 2.78. And he was particularly strong in September, allowing only 8 runs in 30 innings pitched. In addition, he had only given up one homer in the past 2 months. So Walter Alston had confidence in young Roger Craig taking the biggest pitching assignment of the series so far.

The Yankees countered on the mound with 2nd year pitcher, Bob Grim. Grim was the Rookie-of-the-Year in 1954, when he won 20 games, but this year he struggled early and lost his spot in the rotation. As a relief pitcher in August and September, he performed well giving up just 7 earned runs in 28 innings. And with no off days in the World Series, Casey Stengel needed a 5th starter and Grim got the call.

It is most interesting who didn't get the calls to start in yesterday's game, neither the Yankees or Dodgers ace pitchers - Whitey Ford and Don Newcombe.

Ford didn't start because with no days off in this World Series, Casey Stengel was loathe to send out Ford on 3 days' rest as he had not performed well on 3 days' rest during the season.

Newcombe didn't start because he's nursing a sore elbow and needs at least 4 days rest. Suggestions by sportswriters that Newcombe was "dogging it" had Newcombe severely annoyed prior to game 5. Dana Mozley in the New York Daily News noted, ***"Newcombe grabbed a reporter by the arm and took him***

over to his wife sitting in a box behind the screen. Mrs. Newcombe then took off her right glove and showed where her nightly hot towel treatment on Don's sore elbow had chafed her hand."

One more interesting pre-game observation was reported on by Arlie Keller of the Calgary Albertan (that's right, a Canadian newspaper). He observed that Duke Snider hit 5 out of 6 batting practice pitches over the right field screen.

Listen to the Game

You can listen to the game just as I did via the live radio broadcast by searching on YouTube for "1955 10 02 Dodgers vs Yankees World Series Game 5 Complete Radio."

I have provided timestamps for the key moments of the game.

Roger Craig went to a 3 and 2 count on the 1st batter of the game, Elston Howard. On the payoff pitch, he got Howard to swing and miss, eliciting a huge roar from the Ebbets Field crowd. And thus, Roger Craig had a strikeout of the 1st batter he ever faced in World Series competition.

Craig then got Irv Noren to pop up to Pee Wee Reese at shortstop.

After Gil McDougald reached base on an error by Reese, Roger Craig had his 1st stressful moments with Yogi Berra stepping in to the batters' box.

After Yogi swung and missed on a 1 strike count, Craig had the advantage. On the next pitch, Yogi tapped the ball to Gil Hodges at 1st base who stepped on the bag for the 3rd out.

Rookie Roger Craig had pitched a stellar opening inning.

In the bottom of the 1st, Bob Grim took the mound for the 1st time since he had registered the save in game 1. Grim had an easy time. No one hit the ball out of the infield and he retired the side when Campanella was caught looking for a strikeout.

Roger Craig got into a jam to open the 2nd inning as he issued walks to both Joe Collins and Eddie Robinson, running the count to 3 and 2 on both batters. Action started in the Brooklyn bullpen, as Don Bessent began warming up.

Craig got the 1st out when Billy Martin hit a grounder back to him. Craig tossed to Gil Hodges at 1st, but the runners moved up.

Now the Yankees had runners on 2nd and 3rd with 1 out. And this prompted Walter Alston to come out and talk to the infielders.

The next batter, Phil Rizzuto popped up to Gil Hodges in foul territory for out number 2. And that brought up the pitcher, Bob Grim. Grim grounded to Jackie Robinson at 3rd base who threw him out, and Roger Craig was out of the inning without a run scoring.

In the bottom of the 2nd, Carl Furillo lined out to Gil McDougald at 3rd. Then Gil Hodges registered the games' 1st hit with a bloop single into left field.

With 1 out and Hodges on 1st base, Jackie Robinson hit a liner to shortstop Phil Rizzuto who almost doubled up Hodges who slid back just in time.

Now left fielder Sandy Amoros came to the plate. Amoros is a Cuban born player who speaks almost no English and has been in the Dodgers' organization since 1952. He had stellar seasons in AA St. Paul in 1952 and AAA Montreal in 1953 and 1954. He played well enough for the Dodgers in the 2nd half of 1954 that he earned the starting left field job in 1955, but was often platooned so that Junior Gilliam could get time in left field when Don Zimmer played 2nd base. Amoros was 2 for 8 in the series, having started in left field in games 3 and 4.

Now listen to the tape of the game.

At the **40:20 mark,** Al Helfer is on the Mutual Broadcasting System. Helfer was one of the Dodgers' broadcasters along with Vin Scully during the 1955 season. Here is Helfer's call: ***"Two one delivery to Amoros. Curve ball. And Amoros swings on it and gets a hold of it. There's a pretty well jolted ball going deep into right field, it is over the screen out onto Bedford Avenue for a 2-run home run for Sandy Amoros.*** Then Helfer stays quiet for 20 seconds and allows the listeners to hear the extended roar from the crowd.

After the home run, Roger Craig came to the plate. Craig was a poor hitter. In 28 plate appearances he had just 2 hits and 1 walk in his rookie season. But Bob Grim walked Craig.

Craig then moved to 3rd base when leadoff hitter Junior Gilliam singled to right center.

Now there were Dodgers on 1st and 3rd with 2 outs.

But any chance for an extended rally ended when Pee Wee Reese grounded out to 3rd base.

Dodgers 2 Yankees 0 - end of 2 innings

Roger Craig opened the 3rd with his 2nd strikeout of Elston Howard. Then he got Irv Noren to line out to Amoros, and McDougald to ground out to Reese. Roger Craig had his 1st 1-2-3 inning and had completed 3 shutout innings, very impressive for a rookie.

In the bottom of the 3rd, Duke Snider was the 1st batter for the Dodgers. With a count of 1 ball and 2 strikes on the Duke let's listen again to Al Helfer at the **54:28 mark on the tape,** ***"Grim is ready to pitch on the one two count. Rears back. Throws a big curve in there and Duke hits a high drive deep into right field. Collins backs up and watches it. We're watching it too. And it's over the right field screen for a home run for Duke Snider."***

As he did in the prior inning, Helfer goes quiet to let the radio listening audience hear the sustained roar emanating from Ebbets Field fans.

It's Duke's 8th World Series home run, and it ties him with Joe DiMaggio for #3 all-time in World Series history and extends his all-time National League World Series home run record.

Now stay with the tape of the game and at the ***55:40*** **mark** listen just after Irv Noren dives to catch Roy Campanella's line drive, robbing Campy of an extra base hit, ***"Noren really came out of nowhere for that one. He really had to dive. That was the only way he could do it... Boy what a catch by Irv Noren. You like to see competitive spirit like that."***

The catch by Noren was the 1st out of the inning. And Bob Grim stuck out the next 2 batters, Carl Furillo and Gil Hodges to end the inning.

Dodgers 3 Yankees 0 - end of 3 innings

Yogi Berra opened the 4th inning with a bang. Listen to Al Helfer at the **1:00:14 mark**, as Roger Craig throws and Berra, ***"Swings on this pitch and there's a line shot deep to right field, it's up against the scoreboard. Carl Furillo playing it off, fires into second so rapidly that Yogi has to hold onto first with a single, and there's the first hit off of Roger Craig."***

Carl Furillo was a master of the caroms off the right field wall and knew just how to position himself to retrieve the ball and fire it back to the infield. His arm was so feared that he had earned the nickname "The Reading Rifle," after his hometown of Reading, PA.

Holding a runner to 1st base after being hit off the right field wall was a truly incredible feat, but it was a regular occurrence when Carl Furillo played right in Ebbets Field.

Roger Craig got the next batter Joe Collins to strikeout. Then Roger Craig walked Eddie Robinson on a 3 and 2 count. With runners on 1st and 2nd and only 1 out, Don Bessent began warming up again in the Dodgers' bullpen.

Now Billy Martin came up. Listen at the **1:07:26 mark** on the tape to Al Helfer as Craig pitches to Martin, ***"Delivers to the plate, a soft curve. Swung on by Martin. Looped out into left field. It's going to be in there for a base hit. Here comes Sandy Amoros up with the ball. Makes his throw into the plate. Yogi Berra comes in to score."***

The Yankees were on the scoreboard. There were still runners on 1st and 2nd and 1 out. Now Karl Spooner also started warming up in the bullpen for Brooklyn.

Sensing a possible big inning, Casey Stengel decided to pinch hit for shortstop Phil Rizzuto, even though it was just the 4th inning. Moose Skowron came to the plate. Skowron popped up behind home plate to Campanella.

Now with 2 outs Casey let the pitcher, Bob Grim, hit, even though Grim had only batted .120 on the season. He lined out to Reese. The Dodgers had dodged further damage and still led 3 - 1.

In the Dodgers' half of the 4th, Jackie Robinson led off with a walk. After Amoros struck out, Roger Craig sacrificed Jackie over to 2nd base. But the cunning Robinson made a wide turn at 2nd and got exactly what he wanted. He induced Billy Martin, who had covered 1st base, to make an ill-timed throw to the new shortstop Jerry Coleman. Coleman, a utility infielder, had only played 29 games at shortstop in 1955. And just as Robinson must have been envisioning, Coleman wasn't able to handle the throw from Martin. It was classic Jackie Robinson basepath magic, making the other team respond to him and make mistakes, which could lead to runs. But in this case, Robinson wasn't able to take 3rd base as he had already started his slide back into 2nd when Coleman lost the ball.

With 2 outs, and Jackie Robinson on 2nd, Junior Gilliam grounded out to end the 4th inning.

Dodgers 3 Yankees 1 - end of 4 innings

Now Bob Neal took over as the announcer on the Mutual Broadcasting System radio call of the game.

In the 5th, Craig gave up a leadoff hit to Elston Howard, and this prompted action in the bullpen again. But any big threat quickly subsided when Irv Noren hit into a double play. After walking Gil McDougald, Craig got out of the inning when Gil Hodges made a great stop on a hot grounder from Berra. Hodges stepped on 1st and Roger Craig was safely out of another inning. The rookie had allowed just 1 run in 5 innings.

In the bottom of the 5th, Reese grounded out and Duke Snider came to the plate. Listen at **1:30:24 on the tape** as Bob Neal is telling the radio audience about Snider's 3rd inning homer as he waits for Bob Grim to pitch to the Duke with a full count, ***"Duke with his home run has now knocked in 19 runs in World Series competition, for a National League record. Bob Grim is***

ready with the payoff pitch to Snider. He swings, there's a long drive that is going to go (pause) ***way over the wall for a home run."***

Like Al Helfer earlier, Bob Neal goes quiet to allow the microphone to take in the cheers of the Dodgers fans uninterrupted for 20 seconds. Then he continues, ***"The Brooklyn Dodgers have just gone ahead 4 - 1 on a tremendous blast over the right center field wall over on Bedford Avenue by Duke Snider, his second of the ball game, the ninth in this series for the Brooklyn Dodgers. And man, Duke was really smiling when he walked in that dugout. You know both leagues respect Duke as a ballplayer and as a man. He's really something."***

After the homer, Campy walked, and Carl Furillo hit into an inning-ending double play.

Roger Craig was still on the mound for the 6th inning, and he had an easy inning, allowing no hits and only one base runner on a Jackie Robinson throwing error.

In the bottom of the 6th, it was still Bob Grim tossing for the Yankees. Gil Hodges beat out an infield hit, but was out a moment later at 2nd base when Jackie Robinson hit a double play ball. Grim then got Amoros to strikeout making the 6th inning his first time facing just 3 Dodgers.

Dodgers 4 Yankees 1 - end of 6 innings

Bob Grim was the 1st batter due up in the top of the 7th. Casey Stengel decided to pinch hit for Grim and sent Bob Cerv to the plate. Cerv was 0 for 7 in the series so far. But Cerv was a solid hitter. In limited action in 1955, he had batted .341. Cerv immediately helped justify Stengel's nickname, "The Old Professor." He belted a home run into the lower left field stands that pulled the Yankees back to 2 runs down.

Immediately Walter Alston had Clem Labine and Billy Loes begin warming up in the Dodgers' bullpen.

The count went to 3 and 1 on the next hitter, Elson Howard, and that prompted Roy Campanella and Pee Wee Reese to come to the mound to talk to the rookie pitcher, Roger Craig. Craig got the next pitch over for a strike. But then he walked Howard. That alarmed Alston who came out to the mound. After the conversation ran too long, the umpire came to the mound to force the situation. And Alston made the decision to take Roger Craig out. Craig had pitched admirably allowing just 4 hits and 2 runs, although he did walk 5.

The new pitcher was Clem Labine. Labine was making his 4th appearance. He had been in every game except game 3 when Johnny Podres went all the way for the win. And Labine had gotten the win the day before in game 4. Now Labine would be charged with holding the lead.

Labine induced the 1st batter he faced, Irv Noren, to hit into double play from Hodges at 1st to Reese at 2nd and back to Hodges. And then Labine ended the inning by fielding Gil McDougald's smash to the mound and lobbing it to Gil Hodges.

You can hear this great play by Clem Labine at the **1:55:35 mark on the tape.** Listen to Bob Neal say, ***"Here's the 1 - 1 pitch. Swung on. A ground ball caught nicely by Labine. He let's him run. He throws. He's got him. Labine just reached out to the left like a fisherman going in for a big perch."***

I love Bob Neal's imagery in describing Labine's grab of McDougald's grounder.

The Dodgers' half of the 7th saw Bob Turley come in to pitch for the Yankees. Turley had previously pitched in game 3, 2 days earlier as the starter. In that game, Turley lasted just 1 and 1/3 innings as the Dodgers belted him for 4 runs.

Turley's nickname is Bullet Bob. He led the American League in strikeouts last year, in 1954 with 185. This year, in 1955, he had 210 strikeouts. And on this day, his pitches were incredibly fast. He first faced Clem Labine. Labine had hit 3 homers in just 31 at bats in 1955. But against Turley he struck out. After Turley walked Junior Gilliam, next up was Pee Wee Reese, and he struck out looking.

At **2:03:15 on the tape,** Bob Neal says, ***"Mr. Turley is practically knocking the bat out of the batters' hands. He is overpowering them."***

With 2 outs Duke Snider entered the batter's box to face Turley. Duke fouled off the 1st pitch. Then Turley got Duke to swing and miss for strike 2. On the next pitch, Snider hit a fly ball deep down the left field line. It dropped in the corner and Duke Snider ended up on 2nd base with a double.

In his last 3 at bats, Duke Snider had 2 homers and a double.

Now Campanella came to the plate with 2 outs and runners on 2nd and 3rd. This was a chance to really blow open the game. But Turley struck out Campy looking.

Dodgers 4 Yankees 2 - end of 7 innings

Yogi Berra was the leadoff batter in the top of the 8th for the Yankees. He sent Clem Labine's 1st pitch of the inning over the screen atop the 40 foot right field wall, and the ball sailed out onto Bedford Avenue. It was Yogi's 1st RBI of the 1955 World Series. That's quite a remarkable statistic considering that Yogi had led the Yankees in RBIs *every* season going back to 1949, 7 consecutive years. The last time anyone else led the Yankees in RBIs was when Joe DiMaggio knocked in 155 in 1948.

It's pretty remarkable that 5 foot 7 inch Yogi Berra has been the only player to lead the Yankees in RBIs in that entire stretch from 1949 - 1955, when in every single one of those years the Yankees had either Joe DiMaggio or Mickey Mantle starting in center field.

Yogi's homer prodded Alston to have Don Bessent and Billy Loes start working in the bullpen.

Labine got Joe Collins to strikeout swinging on a full count for out number 1.

The next batter, Eddie Robinson also went to a full count. Bob Neal described the action at the **2:12:50 mark** on the tape as Labine prepared to pitch, ***"Labine is ready. And here's the payoff pitch to Robinson. A curve. He drives it out into right field. It's in there for a base hit. Carl Furillo going over near the wall. It bounces off the wall. And Robinson is held at first base***

as Carl Furillo reading every inch of that wood out there gets that ball before it flickers away."

For the 2nd time in the game, Furillo held a Yankees' hitter to a single after a ball had been smashed into the right field wall.

Next up was Billy Martin. With a runner on 1st and 1 out in what was now a 1 run game, this was a tense moment. Listen again to Bob Neal at the **2:15:39 mark on the tape,** ***"The two one pitch to Martin. A ground ball left side, Jackie Robinson in there throws for one, the throw to first. A double play! Hodges hanging on to that ball, had to wait for a moment to make sure he didn't drop it. Umpire Lee Ballanfant watching very carefully, watches as they complete the double play. And it goes 5 to 4 to 3. Robinson to Gilliam to Hodges. And the Dodgers have come up with their 10th double play of the series. Their 3rd of this game... The Dodgers have had superb defensive play."***

Clem Labine had survived the 8th, allowing just a single run on Berra's homer.

In the bottom of the 8th, Carl Furillo led off with a single and Gil Hodges sacrificed him over to 2nd base. Then Jackie Robinson singled to center to drive in a valuable insurance run.

Bob Neal described the reception Robinson received after his run scoring hit at the **2:21:47 mark on the tape,** ***"And Jackie Robinson, as he came back to the Dodger bench was greeted by all of his teammates who have been applauding the performances of the veteran for every game and every inning and every moment of the 5 games of the World Series."***

Jackie Robinson has had a continuous impact on this World Series.

After Jackie's hit, Bob Turley registered 2 more strikeouts, getting Sandy Amoros and Clem Labine to retire the side.

Dodgers 5 Yankees 3 - end of 8 innings

Now the Yankees were down by 2 runs going into their final at bat. Clem Labine came to the mound for his 3rd inning of work. The 1st batter he faced was Andy Carey who was pinch hitting for the shortstop Jerry Coleman. Carey was making his 1st appearance in the series. Carey had been the regular 3rd baseman for most of the season, and led the American League in triples. But he was sent to the bench in September when Billy Martin returned from military service. Martin took his old spot at 2nd base, and Gil McDougald, who played 2nd base most of the season moved to 3rd base.

Labine got Carey to hit a grounder to Jackie Robinson for out number 1.

The 2nd batter was pitcher Tommy Byrne who was sent to pinch hit for Bob Turley. Byrne is an excellent hitter, and Casey had used him as a pinch hitter 18 times during the season. Byrne grounded to Junior Gilliam for out number 2.

The 3rd batter was Elston Howard. He broke his bat sending another grounder to Gilliam, who tossed to Hodges for out number 3.

The Brooklyn Dodgers had won the game and swept the Yankees at Ebbets Field to take a 3 games to 2 lead in the 1955 World Series.

Oh My Darling, Clem Labine

Clem Labine got the save in this game, after getting the win the day before.

At the **2:29:07 mark on the tape,** listen as Bob Neal says, ***"Clem Labine could practically run for a big office in the borough of Brooklyn and be unanimously elected at this moment."***

Indeed Clem Labine was one of the heroes of the game and has been one of the heroes of the Dodgers this entire season as he pitched to a 13 - 5 record and appeared in a league high 60 games as Brooklyn's top relief pitcher.

Syndicated sports columnist Red Smith titled his article on yesterday's game, ***"The Dodgers' Darling Clem Labine."*** In the article he noted that, ***"During the last month of the season writers traveling with the Dodgers began composing a song... it went like this,***

Oh my darling, Clem Labine
Now we need you all the time
For the starters never finish any more.

Honoring the Duke

Red Smith also credited Duke Snider's defensive play in center field as a key to the victory, ***"Snider tearing over the landscape... picking off one howling line drive after another."***

And even Yankees' pitcher Bob Grim had very complimentary things to say about Duke Snider after the game in an interview with Louis Efrat of the New York Times, "***Let me tell you something about Snider's second home run. It was a helluva pitch - a perfect slider, low and on the outside corner. It was one of the best pitches I made all season. But Snider whacked it a mile. His first homer was nothing compared to the second."***

Snider himself was exuberant after the game in which he hit 2 homers to reach 4 for the series, tying the record that he already shared since 1952 with Babe Ruth and Lou Gehrig for most home runs in a single World Series.

But now Snider has done that feat twice, the only one ever to do that.

In addition, by hitting his 9th home run in World Series play for his career, Snider passed Joe DiMaggio to become the 3rd leading World Series home run hitter of all time behind Ruth (15) and Gehrig (10).

Anthony Marenghi of the Newark Star Ledger reported, ***"Standing before his locker after the game - sweaty, tired but quietly jubilant - Snider exclaimed, 'I can't believe it, getting more than DiMaggio. He was always a great inspiration to me and a great ballplayer."***

Duke told Al Wolf of the Los Angeles Times, ***"When I was a kid DiMaggio was my hero. He still is, for that matter. I can hardly realize that I actually went ahead of him today. Gosh, it just doesn't seem possible."***

Not only did Duke pass DiMaggio yesterday, but he did it in just his 23rd World Series game, compared to 51 for DiMaggio. And Gehrig who is just 1 homer ahead of Snider on the all-time World Series HR list played in 34 games.

Casey Stengel also was amazed by Duke Snider's game. He told Will Grimsley of the AP, ***"That fellow was the biggest thing they had out there. Nothing else hurt us - just him. Two home runs and a big double. I blame myself. We oughtn't let a man hit that many home runs on us."***

GAME 6 PREVIEW

The Dodgers, who were down 2 games to none and were being counted out for the series, have now won 3 straight and stand on the precipice of a World Series title.

No team has ever come back from a 2 games to none deficit to win a 7-game World Series. However, no team before the 1955 Dodgers has ever won 3 in a row after dropping the first two.

Now that the Dodgers swept the Yankees in Ebbets Field, they need just 1 more victory over the final 2 games to capture their 1st World Series title.

But those final 2 games will be played in Yankee Stadium where the Dodgers lost games 1 and 2 of this series.

Can the Dodgers win a game in the House That Ruth Built?

And being ahead 3 games to 2 is no guarantee of a World Series victory. Just 3 years ago, in 1952, the Dodgers were ahead 3 games to 2 with the final 2 games of the series at home in Ebbets Field. They couldn't seal the deal. The Dodgers dropped both games at home. Now, here in 1955, they will have to try and win the series on the road.

Chapter Twenty-Four

1955 World Series Game 6 - The Sun Shines on the Dodgers

YANKEE STADIUM, THE BRONX, NY - October 4, 1955

Yesterday, for the 4th time in franchise history, the Brooklyn Dodgers woke up in the morning with the opportunity to win the World Series for the first time.

Each of the 3 prior times they had failed.

They lost in game 7 of the 1947 World Series

They lost game 6 of the 1952 World Series at home when leading 3 games to 2.

They lost in game 7 of the 1952 World Series also at home.

Of course, the opponent each time was the Yankees.

Four Dodgers' players had played in each of those 3 prior potential World Series Championship clinching games. They were Pee Wee Reese, Jackie Robinson, Carl Furillo, and Gil Hodges. Yesterday, that quartet had a chance to avenge the prior misses.

Ahead 3 games to 2, here in the 1955 World Series, a Dodgers victory would result in Brooklyn's first-ever World Series title.

You can listen to the game as I did by searching on YouTube for "October 3 1955 Brooklyn Dodgers At New York Yankees World Series World Series Game 6."

Bob Neal opened the broadcast of game 6 by telling listeners it's a bright sunshiny day. The temperature was 67 degrees and would top 70 during the game.

It was a perfect day to play ball, a perfect day to win the World Series.

Would the sun finally shine on the Dodgers?

The Pitchers

To win the World Series on this day, the Dodgers would have to beat Whitey Ford, the Yankees ace, who had won the 1st game of the series, but did so in unimpressive fashion. Ford would be working on a full 4 days' rest.

But the Dodgers would be unable to counter with their ace, Don Newcombe. Newk was deemed too damaged to start the game. His sore elbow saw him give up an uncharacteristic 4 homers in the game 1 loss, 2 of which were to Joe Collins, a name which most baseball fans are not too familiar.

Walter Alston told an AP reporter that, ***"Newcombe tried to throw in the bullpen yesterday*** (during game 5)***, and they told me he wasn't right, so that's that."***

So instead of the ace, who had been 20 - 5 during the season, the ball went to 24-year-old rookie Karl Spooner, who was 8 - 6 in 1955. The Dodgers were penciling onto the scorecard a 6th different starter in the 6 World Series games. No team had ever done that before.

It would also be the 2nd straight game the Dodgers were starting a rookie on the mound. The day prior, rookie Roger Craig had pitched a strong 6 innings allowing only 2 runs and 4 hits in the game 5 victory.

Before the start of yesterday's game 6, the Dodgers tried to help their batters by enabling them to see similar pitches to Whitey Ford's. Bob Neal told the listening audience that Tom Lasorda, a lefty pitcher from the Dodgers' minor league system, whose style resembles Ford, was asked to drive in 90 miles from his home to throw batting practice in Yankee Stadium. It's likely Lasorda didn't mind the drive.

The 28-year-old Lasorda has been one of the most promising pitchers in the Dodgers' AAA club in Montreal since 1950, compiling a record of 75 - 38 with 13 shutouts. And he might have been on the Dodgers' World Series roster this year if not for the requirement that the bonus baby, Sandy Koufax, have a spot on the roster.

Lasorda had, in fact, started the season with Brooklyn, but was sent back to Montreal on June 8th to make room for Sandy Koufax, who was coming off the disabled list.

Mantle is Out Again

While the Dodgers are missing Newcombe, the Yankees are also missing Mantle again. Mantle has been battling a muscle injury in his leg that prevents him from running. He already missed games 1, 2 and 5. He told the Newark Star-Ledger, ***"There's no use kidding yourself. In my condition, I can't do the team any good."***

Game Time

Lasorda's simulation didn't seem to help Brooklyn in the 1st inning, as Whitey Ford set down the Dodgers in order, getting Duke Snider to go down swinging on a full count to retire the side.

In the bottom of the 1st, Walter Alston was hoping he could get a similar rookie performance out of Karl Spooner as he did with Roger Craig.

The Yankees' leadoff man was Phil Rizzuto. He was the 5th different leadoff batter for the Yankees in the 6 games of the series. Casey Stengel was desperate for

1st inning offense as his team had scored just 1 run in the 1st inning over the 5 prior games in the series.

Rizzuto had the perfect at bat to start the Yankees hitters' first turn. He worked the count to 3 and 2 and then Spooner walked him.

Immediately, Alston must have been 2nd guessing the decision to start another rookie, as he had the injured Don Newcombe begin warming up in the bullpen.

The 2nd batter, Billy Martin, also worked the count full. On the payoff pitch, Rizzuto was running, and while Martin struck out, Rizzuto was safe at 2nd base as Gilliam was late getting to the bag, which forced Campanella to delay his throw. Bill Lee of the Hartford Courant noted that if Gilliam would have covered 2nd base quicker, it would have been a double play.

Instead, Rizzuto was on 2nd with just 1 out. And when Gil McDougald walked, there were Yankees on 1st and 2nd, and still just 1 out.

By this time Karl Spooner had already thrown 17 pitches. And this prompted Alston to have veteran pitcher Russ Meyer begin warming up as well.

Next up was Yogi Berra.

Now listen to the radio broadcast at the **29:25 mark:** Bob Neal says, ***"Rizzuto leads away. The pitch, it's a ground ball by the pitcher, by Gilliam, out into right center field. Here is Rizzuto digging for the plate, going onto 3rd is McDougald. The throw is to 2nd base. And the Yankees break out on top one to nothing. It was a high bouncer that bounced over the outstretched glove of Karl Spooner. It got away, under the reach of Junior Gilliam, who crossed over to his right trying to grab that ball, and it goes into right center field. And Yogi Berra drives in his second run of the World Series."***

The ball had just eluded both Spooner and Gilliam, and now the Yankees were ahead and there was still just 1 out and runners on 1st and 3rd.

Three minutes later, listen at the **32:45 mark** as Hank Bauer is the batter, ***"Here's the two-two pitch. It is swung on. Ground ball to the left side for a base hit. And here is Gil McDougald coming on to score. Berra holds at second. Bauer's on at first, and the Yankees lead two to nothing."***

The ball had made it through the hole between Reese and Robinson. Still 2 Yankee runners on base, still 1 out.

And now it's Moose Skowron at the plate. The 2nd year player is 24 years old and is making just his 2nd World Series start.

The count goes to 2 strikes on Skowron.

Listen again at the 34:40 mark, *"He is pitching to Bill Skowron. Lined into right field. Going over is Carl Furillo. He can't get to it. It's a home run.*

Neal allows the audience to hear the deafening roar in the stadium for the 3-run shot. Then he continues:

"Bill Skowron didn't get around on that ball, but he didn't have to. He hit it out into right field and it carried into the lower stands for a home run. His first World Series home run. And the Yankees now have 5 runs on 3 hits and no errors and there's nobody on, only one man out. And manager Walt Alston is out there to have a chat with Karl Spooner and he's going to make a change. The Yankees erupted with suddenness and ferociousness that was amazing on this fall afternoon."

Skowron's homer wasn't a very long ball. He told Louis Efrat of the New York Times, ***"I just swung with the pitch. He had two strikes on me and I was up there protecting myself. So, when the ball came in to me on the outside, I punched away and it went into the right field seats."***

John Drebinger, also of the Times, noted that Skowron seemed to, ***"chop at the ball."*** Drebinger also indicated, ***"It didn't go very deep... In Ebbets Field it would have hit the fence."***

Skowron had hit into the so-called "short porch" in right field in Yankee Stadium where the line measures just 296 feet.

With the home run, the Yankees had scored five 1st inning runs and knocked the starter, Karl Spooner, out of the game, having gotten just 1 out in 32 pitches.

Alston opted to bring in Russ Meyer. Meyer at age 31, is in his 10th year in the big leagues and pitching in his 3rd World Series. It's his 1st appearance here in the 1955 World Series.

Meyer had pitched a 2-hit shutout in the 4th game of the season in Pittsburgh back in April. But after that he had 5 consecutive outings in which he couldn't get the job done. And by the end of May he had an ERA over 6. After that he had a few spot starts and relief appearances, and never got his ERA back under 5. He finished the season last week with a 3 inning stint back in Pittsburgh in which he gave up just 1 hit and no runs.

Against the Yankees, Meyer gave up an infield hit to the first batter he faced, Bob Cerv, when Meyer failed to cover 1st base on a grounder to Gil Hodgers. But then he struck out Elston Howard and got Whitey Ford to fly out, and the Dodgers' 1st inning nightmare finally concluded.

YANKEES 5 DODGERS 0 - end of 1st inning

In the 2nd inning, neither pitcher gave up a hit.

In the 3rd, Whitey Ford made it 3 straight innings with no Dodgers hits.

In the bottom half of the inning, Meyer allowed a leadoff walk to Berra and a single to Bauer to put men on 1st and 2nd with no outs. Now Moose Skowron came up again with 2 runners on. This time he hit a fly ball to short center field. Racing in, Duke Snider made the grab for the 1st out. Then Meyer got out of the inning when Bob Cerv hit a grounder to Jackie Robinson, who tagged Yogi Berra, the runner heading to 3rd, and threw to Gil Hodges at 1st base for an inning ending double play.

In the top of the 4th, Whitey Ford was charged with his 1st hit of the game when the leadoff batter, Pee Wee Reese, beat the throw to 1st on a high bouncer to Billy Martin.

The next batter was supposed to be Duke Snider, the man who had 4 home runs in the first 5 games of this World Series, and in doing so had become the first player to ever hit that many homers in 2 different World Series. But Walter Alston sent up a pinch hitter, Don Zimmer, to bat for Snider.

Duke Snider was out of the game. The radio announcers didn't know why. But this morning, Myrt Power of INS reported that, ***"Snider hurt his leg when***

he stepped into a hole in the outfield as he was coming in on Skowron's fly ball in the third."

This was an enormous blow for the Dodgers. It was Duke Snider who had supplied much of the Brooklyn's power in the series with 7 RBIs and a .381 average to go along with his 4 clouts. Now they would have to make up a 5-run deficit without the Duke.

Zimmer proved to be no substitute for Snider as he was called out on 3 pitches.

The next Dodger, Roy Campanella, walked on just 4 pitches. Now Brooklyn had runners on 1st and 2nd with 1 out.

Next listen at the **1:12:06 mark on the radio broadcast,** as Carl Furillo is batting against Whitey Ford, ***"The two-two delivery is a curve ball. A ground ball to the left side, hit through into left field. Here's Reese making the turn at third and coming on to score. And Campanella holds at second base.*** (Bob Neal pauses to allow the crowd noise) ***So the Dodgers have chopped one of the five run deficit off and they now trail 5 - 1. And they have two men on with only one man out and the batter is Gil Hodges."***

Gil Hodges came up to the plate. He hit a grounder that got past Gil McDougald at 3rd base, but the shortstop Phil Rizzuto was able to grab it and make the throw to 2nd base just in time to force Furillo.

Now the Dodgers had runners on 1st and 3rd with 2 outs, and Jackie Robinson stepped in.

Bob Neal at **1:13:45 told the listening audience, *"Jackie Robinson, has been a brilliant star for the Brooklyn Dodgers in the field, and has contributed some timely base hits."***

His box score contributions may not have looked stellar. He was 4 for 18 coming into the game. But his contributions in the field, on the base paths, and even at the plate were not going unnoticed. Jackie Robinson, at age 36, was having a strong World Series.

Neal continues at the **1:14:15 mark, *"The pitch to Robinson, swings! And lines one into left field."***

Neal's voice rises as the ball looks for a moment as if it has a chance. He pauses to let the crowd noise in for the listeners, as he and Al Helfer have done after homers. But the ball hooks harmlessly foul.

It seemed for a second like Robinson's smash could've been a 3-run homer, a blast that could have brought the Dodgers right back in the ball game, but instead it was just strike 1 to Jackie.

Prior to the next pitch, Neal says, ***"Remember that song, 'Did you see Jackie Robinson hit that ball?' Well that's what they were thinking about. But he lined it foul. Whitey Ford takes off his cap, thinks to himself, I won't do that again."***

NOTE from The Sports Time Traveler

I interrupt this chapter on game 6 to inform you that I was so intrigued by the reference to a song about Jackie Robinson that I had to search for it. I found it. And you can see a video of Cab Calloway singing the song on the Ed Sullivan show on July 17, 1949 by searching on YouTube for, "Cab Calloway "Did You See Jackie Robinson Hit That Ball?" on The Ed Sullivan Show."

Now back to game 6

On the next pitch, Jackie Robinson grounded out harmlessly to Rizzuto and the side was retired. The Dodgers were still down 5 - 1. But oh, for a second, Dodgers fans thought Jackie Robinson had made the score 5 - 4.

As the Dodgers took the field for the Yankees' half of the 4th inning, there were some changes due to Duke Snider coming out of the game. Sandy Amoros moved from left to center. Jim Gilliam moved from 2nd base to left. And Don Zimmer came in to play 2nd base.

Russ Meyer had an easy inning, as he struck out Howard on 4 pitches and got Whitey Ford and Phil Rizzuto on grounders.

YANKEES 5 DODGERS 1 - end of 4th inning

In the top of the 5th, **listen at 1:23:07** as Sandy Amoros drives a ball into right field. The crowd roars, but the ball, like Robinson's in the last inning, lands in foul territory.

The Dodgers go down quietly and remain down 5 -1 with half the game in the books.

The next several innings were uneventful. Russ Meyer was taken out in the top of the 7th for a pinch hitter. By that time he had pitched a remarkable 5 and 2/3 innings of shutout ball, allowing only 4 hits since bailing out Brooklyn after the disastrous 1st inning. Too bad Meyer hadn't been given the start.

In the 7th and the 8th, yet another rookie pitcher, Ed Roebuck, took the mound for the Dodgers, and he pitched 2 more scoreless innings, allowing just 1 hit. Like Meyer, Roebuck had not seen action in the series prior to game 6.

But Whitey Ford, after surviving the little scare in the 4th, had allowed only 2 hits and no runs in the 5th through 8th innings. And the Dodgers were still in a 5 - 1 hole when they came to the plate in the top of the 9th.

Ford came to the mound in the 9th needing 3 outs to cap off a brilliant pitching performance. The batters due up were Hodges, Robinson and Amoros. This trio had a .373 OBP in the first 5 games. There are really no holes in the Dodgers' lineup. Yet none of them got a ball out of the infield or reached base in the 9th. Whitey Ford needed just 8 pitches to finish off the Dodgers.

Whitey Ford won his 2nd game of this 1955 World Series with a complete game 4-hitter.

Ford's outing was impressive and the greatest hitter in baseball history was in the locker room after the game to tell him so. As reported in today's New York Times, Ty Cobb told Whitey Ford, ***"Son, that was a gorgeous game you pitched. Just perfect. I'd hate to have been hitting against you myself."***

The story of the game was the disastrous 1st inning for the Dodgers, allowing the Yankees to put up 5 runs. Joe Trimble of the New York Daily News wrote this line in the first paragraph of his article, ***"The Brooks, grasping eagerly for***

their first world title, were knocked flat in the first inning at the stadium yesterday as the Yankees put over a five-run stunner."

With the 5 run lead, Whitey Ford took over. Trimble wrote, ***"After that, the game was entirely in the strong left hand of Whitey Ford, and he never faltered."*** What was so surprising for Dodgers fans is that lefty pitchers have won all 3 games for the Yankees, an accomplishment that was supposed to be impossible with the Dodgers' heavy right-handed hitting lineup. Trimble noted that of the Dodgers' 4 hits, ***"Two of the hits were ground balls, and the others were half hit liners."***

Ford explained to Jim McCulley in the Daily News why he was so much more effective yesterday than in game 1, ***"I had what I call my littler sinker. It's a low fastball that breaks down and away from righthanded hitters... But I don't always have that pitch. I'll have it for a couple of games and then lose it... Today it was there and it was my best one."***

The series is now tied at 3 games apiece.

Game 7 will decide the 1955 World Series champion.

Chapter Twenty-Five

1955 World Series Game 7 - Win Now or Wait 'til Next Year

The final game is a legacy making opportunity

YANKEE STADIUM, THE BRONX - October 5, 1955

The Dodgers woke up yesterday with another chance to win the World Series after they had been subdued in game 6.

The momentum in the series which had originally been with the Yankees after they took the opening 2 games in Yankee Stadium, had swung far to the Dodgers' side when the Brooks swept all 3 games at Ebbets Field. But back in the Stadium for game 6, the Yankees' 5 run 1st inning burst, knocked out the rookie pitcher Walter Alston had sent to the mound. And combined with Whitey Ford's lock-down pitching, the momentum has swung back to the Bronx Bombers as they took game 6 in a contest that was never close.

But Dodgers' captain, Pee Wee Reese, remained confident. He penned an article in the Newark Star-Ledger that appeared yesterday morning, prior to game 7, in which he declared, ***"We are far from disheartened. We expect to win."***

One reason to believe for the Dodgers is that 23-year-old Johnny Podres, who won game 3 on his birthday, was selected to pitch game 7. Podres, bolstered by his great performance in game 3, made bold claims about what he would do on the mound in the decisive contest.

In Reese's article in the Star-Ledger, he noted that Johnny Podres told him, ***"I'm the boy tomorrow. I'll do it right up for us."***

Carl Lundquist of the UPI reported Podres saying the day before game 7, ***"My arm is loose and limber. Last time I celebrated my birthday. Tomorrow it will be everybody's birthday."***

Jimmie Fleming in the New Brunswick Home News had heard Podres tell Pee Wee Reese, after manager Alston had notified him he was pitching game 7, ***"I'll shut 'em out."***

The Dodgers Ace is Out

Although the Dodgers had confidence in young Johnny Podres, they had to feel they were sorely missing their sore-armed ace, Don Newcombe. While Podres was just 9 - 10 for the entire 1955 campaign, Newk had been the best pitcher in baseball over the first 4 months of the season. His won-loss record stood at a historic level, 18 - 1, on July 31st after he beat the Cardinals in St. Louis on 5 hits.

There was every reasonable expectation in mid-season that Don Newcombe would be good for 2 victories in the World Series.

But a sore arm and shoulder plagued Newk for the final 2 months of the season. Newcombe's ERA for the month of September was an abysmal 5.23 in 3 starts. Earlier in the year, his season ERA had dipped as low as 2.50 when he beat the Braves on June 25th to record his 13th win against 1 loss.

Newk gave it a try in game 1 of the World Series, but was shelled for 4 homers in less than 6 innings in the 6 - 5 loss.

Don Newcombe's sore arm and shoulder created a murky mess for manager Walter Alston who had to juggle veterans and rookies without his ace starter available for the rest of the series.

Newk lamented to Lundquist the day before game 7, ***"I can't pitch tomorrow either unless a miracle occurs."***

Even though it was apparent that Newcombe could not deliver a solid performance in game 7, many thought the Dodgers should go to their ace for the decisive contest. Stanley Woodward of the Star-Ledger noted that, ***"there are uncontrolled second-guessers who think Walter Alston may forego this selection*** (of Podres as the starter) ***at the last minute and come in with Don Newcombe... Newcombe claims he wants to pitch, though he says his arm is sore. This combination of desire and neurosis leaves poor old Alston on the spot. Whatever he does, he will be wrong unless his team wins."***

Such is life for a manager in the World Series.

Alston stuck with Johnny Podres as his starter.

The Yankees Turn to Byrne

Casey Stengel had a much easier choice for his starting pitcher for game 7. Tommy Byrne had been brilliant in game 2, going the distance and defeating the Dodgers on 5 hits. The 35-year-old Byrne had been a reliable starter since the end of May and held the Yankees' best won-loss record in 1955 at 16 - 5. Now with 4 days' rest, Tommy Byrne was ready to shut down the Dodgers again and deliver yet another World Series title for the Yankees.

Jackie, Mickey and the Duke

Three of the biggest stars were injured going into game 7.

One of the longest tenured Dodgers on the team, Jackie Robinson, was declared out for game 7. Jackie had played in 31 consecutive World Series games with the team going back to the 1947 World Series. But now Jackie was suffering with a painful right heel injury that restricted his mobility in the field.

Robinson told Joseph Sheehan in the New York Times, ***"I could play, but Don Hoak will do a much better job for us. With my heel the way it is, I just can't make a quick start and I wouldn't have a chance on any ball that wasn't hit right at me."***

He told the Star-Ledger, ***"I want to play if I can help the club. It's up to Walt*** (Alston).***"***

The Yankees also had a star player who could not start the game. Center fielder Mickey Mantle, unable to run with a muscle tear, had been in just 2 games in the series and was not in the starting lineup again yesterday.

Mickey's replacement in center field, Bob Cerv, was hitting just 2 for 12 (.167) for the series.

Mantle told the Newark Star-Ledger after game 6, ***"There's no use kidding yourself, in my condition I can't do the team any good."***

Dodgers' center fielder, Duke Snider, was doubtful for game 7 after he injured his knee stepping in a hole in center field in Yankee Stadium in game 6. He had to come out of that game.

But the Duke told Dick Young of the New York Daily News after game 6, ***"If I can walk, I will play."***

And yesterday afternoon, a limping Duke was in the starting lineup.

A Game for the Ages

The front page of the New York Daily News yesterday summed up the stakes for game 7 with a banner headline, ***"All Even: One Game Does It."***

Game 7 was set to be a thriller.

Oddsmakers had the Yankees as a 7 to 5 favorite likely because every game had been won by the home team and game 7 was in Yankee Stadium.

And the oddsmakers had been right in each of the first 6 games.

Listen to the Game

You can experience the final game of the 1955 World Series the same way I did by listening to the Mutual Broadcasting System radio call of the game. You can find it on YouTube by typing this in the search bar, "**1955 10 04 World Series Game 7 Dodgers vs Yankees.**"

One of the Dodgers' regular announcers, Al Helfer, was on the play-by-play to start the game.

I have provided my commentary on the game with time stamps from the radio broadcast.

10:20 - Tommy Byrne delivers the first pitch of the game to Junior Gilliam, and it's a called strike.

On Byrne's 2nd pitch, Gilliam hits a bouncer that shortstop Phil Rizzuto handles and there's one down.

Dodgers' shortstop, Pee Wee Reese flies out to Mantle's replacement Bob Cerv in center field for the 2nd out.

Next up is Duke Snider. The Duke gets a huge applause when he comes to the plate in Yankee Stadium. It sounds like a large portion of the crowd is rooting for Brooklyn. Snider has hit 4 home runs in the series. But in this at-bat, he grounds out to 2nd baseman Billy Martin.

Tommy Byrne is off to an outstanding start, he threw a strike on the 1st pitch to each batter and retired the side in order on just 6 pitches.

13:40 - Al Helfer tells the listening audience that Phil Rizzuto is playing his 52nd World Series game, breaking Joe DiMaggio's record for most games played.

17:32 - After Podres has gotten Phil Rizzuto to pop up to the catcher, Roy Campanella, and has retired Billy Martin on a fly ball down the left field line, he runs the count full on 3rd baseman Gil McDougald. Here is Helfer's call on the payoff pitch, ***"Podres ready. Here's his 3 and 2 delivery. Slow curve for a called strike 3."***

There's a huge roar. It sounds as if the majority of the crowd is pulling for 'Dem Bums.

Podres has set the Yankees down in order on 11 pitches.

YANKEES 0 DODGERS 0 - end of 1st inning

Tommy Bryne throws his first ball out of the strike zone to open the 2nd inning to Roy Campanella. Then Campy grounds out to Martin on the 2nd pitch.

Next, Carl Furillo flies out to left on the 1st pitch. There are 2 down.

But Gil Hodges walks on 4 pitches. The Dodgers' 1st baseman since 1948 becomes the game's 1st base runner.

Next up is Jackie Robinson's replacement at 3rd base, Don Hoak. This is Hoak's 1st ever at-bat in a World Series game. He goes down on a slow roller to Billy Martin for the 3rd out.

Tommy Byrne is looking sensational through 2 innings.

In the bottom of the 2nd, Yogi Berra leads off. Berra leads all batters in this World Series with 9 hits. And he's batting .450 for the series (9 for 20).

25:39 - Listen to Al Helfer and hear the crowd roar on this play, ***"Podres tries the curve, and it's swung on, hit out to centerfield. Duke Snider limping over under, and makes the catch."***

The play-by-play in the Atlantic City Press indicated it was a running catch by the injured Snider. The Duke is giving it everything he's got.

Podres next gets Hank Bauer to swing on one of his slow pitches, and he grounds the ball to Don Zimmer at 2nd base. Two outs.

The next batter is Bill "Moose" Skowron. Podres gets 2 strikes on Skowron. After the 2nd strike, a frustrated Moose throws his bat, nearly hitting Yankees' 3rd base coach Frankie Crossetti.

27:14 - Listen to Helfer on the next pitch from Podres, ***"Fastball. Swung on by Skowron. Drilled out along the right field line. It bounces and up into the crowd for an automatic two-bagger."***

Moose is on 2nd base with the 1st base hit of game 7.

Next Bob Cerv comes to the plate. Mantle's replacement is hitting just 2 for 12 in the series, but 1 of the 2 hits was a home run.

Cerv swings and misses on a 1st ball fastball.

28:19 - Al Helfer calls the next pitch, ***"Podres ready with the 0, 1 delivery. Checks the runner Skowron. Delivers to the plate a soft curve. swung on and missed for strike 2. Cerv lost his bat on that one. Podres set him up with the fastball and then fired that low, tantalizing curve on him, and Cerv was way out ahead of it."***

On the next pitch, Cerv hits a grounder to Reese and Podres is out of the 2nd inning.

In the top of the 3rd inning, the Dodgers go down quietly again. Byrne yielding just a walk to Junior Gilliam.

In the last of the 3rd, Elston Howard is fooled by a Podres change up and flies out to center.

Next up is the pitcher, Tommy Byrne. He's a good hitter, who was actually used as a pinch hitter earlier in the series. He gets the count to 3 - 0. Then he takes 2 pitches for called strikes and fouls off a pitch.

Now Byrne is set to receive his 7th pitch from Podres, more than any other Yankee so far.

42:18 - Here is Al Helfer's call as Podres throws with a full count, ***"3, 2 pitch. Called strike 3! Drilled right through the middle at the knees."*** The crowd roars at the strikeout, which is the 2nd out of the inning for the Yankees. It's remarkable how many Dodgers fans are inside Yankee Stadium.

The next batter, Rizzuto, walks on 4 pitches.

With 2 outs, Billy Martin steps in. The first pitch is a ball. The 2nd pitch is a slow curve in the dirt for ball 2.

Johnny Podres appears to be having control problems and Don Bessent starts to warm up in the Dodgers' bullpen.

Then Podres finally throws a strike after 6 consecutive balls.

46:00 - Listen to the call on the 2 and 1 pitch, ***"Podres checks his runner. Delivers. Martin swings. Hits a ball out into right field. It's going to be in for a base hit. Furillo comes along, picks it up. And Rizzuto holds at second."***

Rizzuto doesn't think about trying for 3rd base on Carl Furillo. But the Yankees have runners on 1st and 2nd. And that brings Walter Alston to the mound to talk to his 23-year-old starter.

After Alston is finished talking to his young hurler, Podres continues his control issues as Gil McDougald takes 2 slow curves for balls. After a strike on the 3rd pitch, Podres throw a soft curve for a ball. It's a 3 and 1 count with runners on 1st and 2nd and 2 outs.

The next pitch is hit foul, and it's a full count.

Now listen to Helfer.

50:00 - ***"Count on McDougald three balls and two strikes. Two down last half of the third, no score. The Yankees own the only 2 base hits in the ball game. Johnny Podres, a great big heave and a sigh on the mound. Goes to the top of the stretch. Checks his runners, particularly Rizzuto at second. The pitch is made as the runners break. Hit down to Hoak at third.*** (the crowd roars) ***And the ball hits the runner. Hits the runner, Phil Rizzuto. So that is going to be the third out in the inning."***

It's a huge break for Brooklyn, and Podres is out of a jam. Side retired.

Don Hoak was behind Rizzuto as the ball bounded just inside the 3rd base line. Hoak did not have a play on the ball before it hit Rizzuto, who had nearly reached 3rd base before he was hit by the ball.

If Rizzuto had avoided being hit, he certainly would have been safe at 3rd base, as photos of the play in the New York Times today revealed.

It's a big blow for the Yankees. If Rizzuto was not hit by the ball, he might have scored if Hoak couldn't handle it and it went into left field. At worst, the Yankees would have had bases loaded for Yogi Berra, their leading RBI man.

Instead, Podres gets out of a tough inning in which his control was shaky, and he had to throw 23 pitches.

McDougald got credit for a single even though he hit into the 3rd out.

YANKEES 0 DODGERS 0 - end of 3rd inning

The crowd roars as Duke Snider strikes out swinging to begin the 4th. So there are in fact Yankees fans in the stadium.

Now listen to Al Helfer on the call with Roy Campanella at the plate.

54:20 - ***"The 1, 0 delivery to Campanella. Swung on. There's a line drive hit over third base down in the corner. Campanella is down to second*** (Helfer means that Campy has made the turn past 1st base). ***Elston Howard comes up with the ball. Campy's going to keep on going. The ball gets away from Howard. And Campy moves into second."***

It's credited as a double and it's the Dodgers' 1st hit of the game.

Next up is Carl Furillo, On the 1st pitch, Furillo drills a long ball down the left field line that hooks foul. It has the Dodgers fans in the crowd roaring for a second.

Listen as Al Helfer shares with the audience how close it was to a 2-run homer.

55:35 - ***"That had the distance. But was pulled too much. That sort of electrified everybody here at Yankee Stadium."***

Furillo then takes 3 balls, and it's a 3 - 1 count. Then he hits another line shot foul, and the count is full to Furillo.

But on the next pitch, Furillo grounds out to 2nd. Campy moves to 3rd with 1 out.

Now Casey Stengel comes out to talk to Tommy Byrne with Gil Hodges coming up to the plate.

Listen as the count on Gil Hodges is 1 ball and 2 strikes.

1:02:14 - ***"Yankee pitcher checks his runner at third, Campanella. Delivers one and two to the plate to Hodges. Fastball. Swung on. Hit out into left field. It's in for a base hit. Roy Campanella comes home to score. The Brooks lead it one to nothing."***

There is considerable cheering as the Dodgers strike first and lead the game 1 to nothing.

There's no rally however as Hoak grounds out to 3rd for the final out.

In the bottom of the 4th, Yogi Berra leads off.

Helfer makes the call on the 2nd pitch to Berra.

1:05:50 - ***"Fastball and Yogi after it. Hits a high pop up out into center field. Coming over to it is Jim Gilliam. Duke Snider's there. And they both allow the ball to drop. Yogi Berra winding up at second."***

It was a communication problem as both men were coming for the ball. Snider had to back off so he didn't run into Gilliam. And then Gilliam backed off too. After the game, Snider took responsibility for the mishap. It's likely that Gilliam was coming for the ball under the assumption that Snider's faulty knee might not enable him to make the play.

Whatever the case, the Yanks have a leadoff runner for the 1st time in the game, and he's in scoring position.

The next batter, Hank Bauer flies out to Furillo in right on the 1st pitch and Berra holds at 2nd.

Then Moose Skowron grounds to Zimmer. Berra moves to 3rd on the play with 2 outs.

Now Bob Cerv is at bat, and Podres gets him to pop up. Pee Wee Reese calls everyone off, there's going to be no mishaps on this play. The Dodgers' captain,

Pee Wee Reese, catches the ball to retire the side. Berra has been stranded at 3rd. And young Johnny Podres has made it through 4 innings unscathed.

DODGERS 1 YANKEES 0 - end of 4th inning

Don Zimmer is called out on strikes leading off the 5th.

The next batter is Podres. He gets a nice applause as he approaches the plate for a short-lived trip as he pops up on the 1st pitch.

Byrne ends an easy inning as he gets Gilliam on a grounder to Martin at 2nd.

To start the Yankees' half of the 5th inning, Al Helfer turns over the microphone to Bob Neal. In parting, Helfer informs the listening audience that Neal is suffering from a cold. But as Neal begins, you can't hear anything but vigor in his voice.

Now listen to Bob Neal.

1:15:55 - On the 1st pitch that Neal calls there is action. He raises his voice as he makes the call, ***"Elston Howard steps in. Podres, the left-hander delivers. There's a drive deep to left field. Going back for it is Junior Gilliam. Still going back. He reaches up. He's got it. And Elston Howard really started to warm things up quickly as he drives deep to Junior Gilliam in front of the wall out in left field. Well that shook up a few folks including Johnny Podres who heaves a couple of big sighs to make sure he's still breathing. Because Elston Howard made a bid to tie up this ball game."***

Johnny Podres has survived a close call on Howard's drive to deep left.

Now listen to Neal again as the pitcher, Tommy Byrne comes to the plate.

1:17:35 - ***"So Johnny Podres, who is 23-years-old, working out there as if he had ice water running through his veins. And he's pitching to another veteran who has pitched outstanding ball not only in this game, but in his other performance."***

Podres strikes out Byrne looking for the 2nd out. And then Rizzuto grounds out.

It's an easy side for Podres, but it was oh so close to being a tie ball game.

In the top of the 6th, Reese hits a liner over the head of shortstop Phil Rizzuto for a leadoff single.

Duke Snider lays down a beautiful bunt that stops around 10 feet from the plate. Tommy Byrne gets to it and whips the ball to Skowron at 1st base. However Skowron had been moving in on the bunt attempt, and he can't quite get back to the bag. His only option is to tag Snider.

But Snider bumps Skowron's arm, and the ball pops out. Everyone is safe.

The Dodgers have runners on 1st and 2nd and no outs with the clean-up hitter Campanella due up.

Bob Grim starts to warm up in the Yankees' bullpen.

Now Walter Alston has Campy bunt. Two of the most dangerous hitters in baseball have just laid down bunts to Byrne. Byrne again grabs the bunt and throws to 1st. Martin covers the bag, and Reese and Snider move up to 2nd and 3rd with 1 out.

The mighty Dodgers' hitters are playing small ball in this tight game.

Casey Stengel comes out to the mound. He leaves Byrne in the game.

Casey decides to walk Carl Furillo to load the bases for Gil Hodges.

It's Reese on 3rd, Snider on 2nd, Furillo on 1st and Hodges at the plate.

How many games had this quartet played together? And here they were in one of the biggest games of their lives, all on the bases at the same time and with just 1 out.

But before a pitch is thrown, Casey Stengel comes back to the mound again, and this time he decides to remove Byrne and bring in Bob Grim.

The 1st pitch by Grim is a fastball for a strike. The next is a curve outside. The count is 1 and 1.

Now listen to Bob Neal describe the action.

1:31:22 - ***"Here's the 1, 1 pitch. It's a curve ball hit out to right center field. Going over is Bob Cerv. Still going over. And he reaches up. He makes the catch. And here comes Pee Wee Reese. The throw comes in to second base, and Snider goes to third. And the Dodgers lead two to nothing."***

Gil Hodges has now driven in both of Brooklyn's runs. And the Dodgers take a 2 - 0 lead.

Don Hoak is up next and he walks to load the bases again with 2 outs.

But there is no further damage as pinch hitter George Shuba, hitting for Don Zimmer, grounds out to 1st base to end the threat.

The Double Switch

With Don Zimmer out of the game, Walter Alston makes a double switch. He moves Junior Gilliam in from left field to take Zim's place at 2nd base. And he inserts Sandy Amoros into left field.

The purpose of all this is to ensure that Alston has lefty hitters in the lineup to face Grim, a righty pitcher, after the lefty Byrne had been removed from the game. Junior Gilliam is a switch hitter, and Sandy Amoros throws and bats lefty.

As the bottom of the 6th begins, Billy Martin walks on 4 pitches, and this brings Walter Alston to the mound again. He has Don Bessent again start warming up, and this time he also has Clem Labine start tossing in the bullpen as well.

Now the Yankees play small ball, too. The 3rd batter in the lineup, Gil McDougald, bunts along the 3rd base line.

Podres's throw is late.

The Yankees have men on 1st and 2nd and no outs.

Berra at the plate now represents the go ahead run. Yogi Berra, the Yankees top RBI man in each of the past 7 seasons, can tie the game with an extra base hit.

The first pitch from Podres is a ball.

Now listen to Neal's call on the 2nd pitch to Berra.

1:41:35 - *"The outfield is around to the right. Duke Snider in right center. Carl Furillo deep in right field. Hodges playing even with first and playing in front of the runner. The pitch is swung on. A fly ball hit into left field. Junior Gilliam who was pulled around going hard, heading*

way over near the foul line. He reaches up and he's got the ball. And the throw to first. And they have Gil McDougald doubled.

Neal is mistaken on the call. It's Sandy Amoros playing left who had taken Gilliam's place when Gilliam moved to 2nd base.

Sandy Amoros had been shifted over towards center against the lefty hitting Berra. But the ball was sliced down the left field line. Amoros had to run a 60 yard dash to get to the ball, and he makes a one-handed grab on the run just before the wall.

It's a sensational catch.

The New Brunswick Home News wrote this morning, ***"The catch made by Amoros in the sixth will go down with the greatest in World Series history."***

Neal continues his call as he recaps this incredible defensive gem, ***"The relay man was Pee Wee Reese so it goes 7, 6, 3. And there's two outs and Billy Martin's on second and the Dodgers are protecting their two run lead... Great defensive play by Sandy Amoros who defied all odds by making the catch and then alertly pumping that ball into Reese who fired it over to first base to double off Gil McDougald... I don't believe a right-handed outfielder could have made a catch of that ball that was hit by Yogi Berra. Sandy Amoros using his left hand as an aid, reached right in the corner and just got his glove on it.***

You can see the play in a video on YouTube titled, "The Greatest Double Play in World Series History."

The next batter, Hank Bauer grounds out to Reese, and what could have been a big Bronx Bombers' inning has been shut down.

Whew! What a close call for Podres and the Dodgers.

And what a sensational play by both Amoros and Reese. Both of them needed to make perfect throws to double up McDougald and they did.

DODGERS 2 YANKEES 0 - end of 6th inning

Johnny Podres is the leadoff man in the top of the 7th. Listen to Bob Neal as Podres comes up.

1:47:37 - ***"Johnny Podres getting a big hand as he comes up there. This young fellow has certainly exhibited great courage."***

Podres grounds out to Martin.

The next batter, Junior Gilliam singles to right. But he's out trying to steal second.

And a moment later, Pee Wee Reese strikes out.

It's short work for Grim.

In the bottom of the 7th, Skowron leads off with a grounder to Reese.

The Brooklyn Dodgers are now 8 outs away from a World Series title. This is the 1st time in franchise history they have ever been this close.

The Dodgers have never before been 8 outs away. They were 9 outs away in game 6 of the 1952 World Series before the Yankees came back to win that game handily 5 - 2.

The next batter Cerv, grounds out to Reese as well. 7 outs to a title.

Bob Neal now describes why Johnny Podres has been so effective on this day.

1:55:09 - ***"Johnny Podres comes in with that let up pitch just as if he's coming in with that fastball. About three-quarters. And having the same delivery kind of fools 'em."***

But Podres doesn't fool the next batter, Elston Howard. He smashes a ball through the left side, and Reese dives but can't get it.

After Howard reaches safely, there is a loud cheer. Bob Neal describes the action.

1:55:57 - ***"And Mickey Mantle is going to bat for Bob Grim. Mickey Mantle, who has certainly been handicapped with muscle problems, has been in only two games. He's been at bat nine times. He has two hits, one home run, one RBI."***

The home run that Neal mentions was hit off Podres in game 3.

A home run here would tie the game.

This is yet another dangerous situation, perhaps the most dangerous of the game for the Dodgers. This is Mickey Mantle. And he's hit a home run in 5 of the past 10 World Series games he's played in going back to 1952.

The 1st pitch from 23-year-old Podres to 23-year-old Mantle is hit foul.

The 2nd pitch is one of Podres's let up curves. It's outside, according to Neal.

The 3rd pitch is a fastball. And Mickey pops it up. Reese grabs it.

The inning is over.

The Dodgers need 6 more outs to win the World Series. They are in uncharted territory.

The 8th Inning

Bob Turley comes in to pitch for the Yankees. The 1st batter he faces is Duke Snider and he strikes him out on a fastball that popped away from the Duke, according to Neal.

Next up, Campanella swings and misses badly on the 1st pitch. Turley has thrown 4 straight strikes to open the inning.

Neal indicates the shadows are making it hard to see the ball. On the next pitch, Campy flies out. And then Furillo flies out to center.

It's on to the bottom of the 8th. And young Johnny Podres is still out there throwing.

Phil Rizzuto leads off with a single to left center.

The tying run is at the plate with Billy Martin.

Listen to Neal call the action.

2:06:41 - *"The pitch to Martin. A swing and a slasher going out to right field. Coming hard is Carl Furillo. He's got it... Carl Furillo coming from deep right field... Furillo makes a good grab, belt high and held on to it."*

It's yet another great defensive play. If Furillo doesn't get to the ball, the Yankees would have had men on 1st and 3rd with no outs and the go ahead run at the plate with the power hitters coming up.

Now Gil McDougald is up with Rizzuto on 1st base and 1 out.

The count goes to 3 and 2. Neal describes the payoff pitch.

2:09:31 - ***"Here's the pitch. There he goes*** (Rizzuto is running). ***Swing. A ground ball left side. Bounces off Hoak's shoulder it goes out into left field. It's a base hit. Here's Rizzuto going to third... So Gil McDougald gets credit for a base hit. That ball took a bad hop, hit Don Hoak in the shoulder and the Yankees have the tying runs on bases."***

It's trouble again for Podres, with runners on 1st and 3rd and just 1 out.

Alston comes out to talk to the youngster who has now given up his 8th hit.

The Dodgers are clinging to a 2 - 0 lead.

Walter Alston leaves Podres in the game.

Now Podres faces Yogi Berra. Berra had nearly hit a home run in his last time up. The crowd is starting to ***"whip it up now,"*** Neal says.

The count goes to 3 and 0. A walk would put the go ahead run on base.

Berra gets wood on the 3 and 0 pitch from Podres. But it's just a pop up to short right. It's an easy one for Carl Furillo. But with Rizzuto at 3rd base, there was the potential for him to score.

The Home News reported what happened next, ***"Furillo whipped the ball into home on a perfect peg."***

There was zero chance for Rizzuto to tag up on Carl Furillo with his rifle arm.

Now with 2 outs and runners on 1st and 3rd, Hank Bauer steps in. Bauer is 6 for 13 for the series (.461). He's the hottest hitter in the series, but he hasn't had a single hit off Podres. Bauer was 0 for 4 in the series to this point against Podres.

In between pitches to Bauer, Bob Neal took a moment to share his thoughts about young Johnny Podres.

2:12:12 - ***"Regardless of who wins this game, you must salute Johnny Podres and his great heart and courage... Johnny Podres, pitching his heart out for his Brooklyn Dodgers and trying to help his team win their first World Series engagement."***

Then, with the count on Bauer at 2 and 2, Neal calls the action.

2:13:11 ***"It's two and two. Outfield straight away. Rizzuto at third. McDougald at first. The pitch to Bauer. Swing and a miss! He strikes him out. No runs for the Yankees. Two hits. There were no errors, and two men were left on. And Johnny Podres could run for mayor of Brooklyn, and I think almost the area around Yankee Stadium, and be elected unanimously."***

After the strikeout the cheers are as loud as they've been the entire game.

The New Brunswick Home News reported that Bauer, ***"went down swinging on a shoulder-high fast ball, probably the hardest pitch Podres made all day."***

The Dodgers have 3 outs to go to win a World Series for the 1st time.

The Top of the 9th Inning

Gil Hodges leads off the Dodgers' 9th with a pop up.

Don Hoak then gets his 1st ever World Series hit with a single to right.

Sandy Amoros draws a walk, and now the Dodgers have a legitimate scoring threat with runners on 1st and 2nd and just 1 out.

The next batter is Podres, and he receives a huge ovation. Neal describes it.

2:20:10 - ***"And the hand is for Johnny Podres. Just listen to it."***

Podres flies out to Cerv in center.

Junior Gilliam comes up with 2 outs and he hits a long fly ball. It's deep in right center. But Bauer is able to haul it in. For a second, it looked like a series clinching 3-run shot.

So the game goes to the bottom of the 9th with the Dodgers clinging to their 2 - 0 lead.

Dodgers fans must hold their breath. Just 4 years ago the prior day, the Dodgers held a 3 run lead in the bottom of the 9th against the Giants in the pennant playoff finale, and lost when Bobby Thomson hit his legendary homer.

Bottom of the 9th

The Yankees are down to their final at bat unless they can score at least 2 runs. The Dodgers are clinging to a slim 2 - 0 lead.

The kid, Podres, is still pitching.

The first Yankees' hitter is Bill Skowron. He's 1 for 3 in this game, and 3 for 7 for the series. All of his hits have been off Podres.

The 1st pitch is low for ball 1.

The 2nd pitch is a curve that's in there for a strike.

The 3rd pitch is low again for ball 2. It's 2 balls and 1 strike to Skowron.

The 4th pitch is another curve. It catches the inside corner and the count is now 2 and 2. Listen to Bob Neal describe Podres's curve ball.

2:24:35 - ***"That ball broke about four feet."***

Now listen again as Neal describes the next pitch.

2:25:01 - ***"The swing and a ground ball right back. Podres grabs the ball and tosses underhanded to the first baseman, and apparently he had trouble digging the ball up out of his glove. But he gets it over in time."***

Two outs to go.

Next up is Bob Cerv who is hitless in 3 times at the plate. The 1st two pitches are fastballs for a strike and a ball. The 3rd pitch is yet another fastball for a strike. The crowd roars.

Listen to Bob Neal after the strike on the 3rd pitch to Cerv.

2:26:15 - ***"That young Podres seems to be throwing just as hard now as he was in the first inning."***

On the next pitch, Cerv pops up to short left field. Amoros makes the catch.

One out to go.

Elston Howard steps in. Howard had hit a home run in his 1st World Series at bat back in game 1. But he's only 3 for 20 since then.

Howard takes a called strike on the 1st pitch.

The next pitch is a curve outside for a ball.

Neal describes the scene before the next pitch.

2:27:28 - ***"The fans are standing up because all of the excitement, all of the great pitching, all of the power, all of the defensive ability is tied in now, and all attention is focused now on this youngster with the left arm who deals in... swings and misses. One and two."***

Podres had thrown the pitch as Neal was giving his speech about Podres.

And now the Dodgers need one more strike to win the World Series.

Neal continues... ***"So Johnny Podres now has a one ball, two strike count on Elston Howard. And we have two out in the last half of the ninth inning. And the Brooklyn Dodgers are leading two to nothing. The Yankees are playing in Yankee Stadium and the Dodgers are leading two to nothing. That in itself is historical. Podres now with the double wind up. The one, two pitch, Howard takes high. Ball two. Two balls, two strikes."***

I find it hard to imagine the stress felt by 26-year-old Elston Howard as he looks at a pitch in this situation. If it had been called a strike, it would have ended the World Series with him looking at one go by him.

Neal continues.

"And you know, you really have to pay a compliment to the umpires. Men who must make decisions quickly. And who are watching carefully every pitch. Two balls, two strikes, with two out and Johnny Podres nods his head to Roy Campanella. He's into a double wind up. The outfield straight away. Triple wind up. And Elston Howard decides to step out and does."

The tension for the Dodgers, and Dodgers fans must be terrific.

Neal speaks again.

"Now umpire Jim Honochick moves back of the plate. He motions to Johnny Podres, it's alright. Johnny Podres heaves a great big sigh. He looks in. He starts the pump. And the two, two pitch is swung on and fouled back. It's two and two."

Howard is making the best of his at bat, and he gets a piece of a ball and will see another pitch.

Neal picks it up again.

"Two balls, two strikes. Yankee Stadium, scene of many historic battles, of all sports events, is being thrilled here at the moment. Here's the two, two delivery. A swing and a foul. And it goes into the upper deck."

Yet another chance for Howard.

Neal continues his radio call.

"So the mantle of greatness which is being held by only fate alone waiting for Johnny Podres to step in and have it hoisted on his shoulders. And he very casually pulls his socks up. Now he looks into Roy Campanella. Nobody on, two out. The Dodgers leading two to nothing. This the last half of the ninth inning."

Imagine now what Podres is thinking. He's pitched a great game. But he still has to finish it off.

Neal describes the next pitch.

"Johnny Podres into his windup and the two, two pitch, a let up curve. A ground ball to the left side. Pee Wee Reese has it. The throw to first. And he's out. And the Dodgers win by a score of two to nothing. Fine play by Pee Wee Reese and out in front of the mound they're grabbing Johnny Podres, they're pummeling him, pushing him around. The final score is Dodgers two runs, five hits, no errors. The Yankees no runs, eight hits and one error."

The Brooklyn Dodgers had done it! They'd won the World Series, their 1st ever World Series. And they did so in spectacular fashion, shutting out their nemesis, the Yankees, in Yankee Stadium. And holding the Yankees scoreless, in Yankee Stadium, for the final 16 innings!

And in a fitting finish to it all, it was Pee Wee Reese making the play on the final out. Reese is the only Dodger to have played on all five prior Dodgers' teams that lost the World Series to the Yankees, going back to his rookie season of 1941.

And it was also fitting that Gil Hodges made the final putout. Hodges has been on the roster since 1947 and in his quiet manner, the sturdily built Hodges has been the backbone of the Boys of Summer.

Bill Corum now comes on the radio broadcast to recap the finish.

2:30:32 - ***"This was as fine a World Series ball game as ever has been played almost. And certainly nobody ever pitched a more stealth hearted one than Johnny Podres... who stood out there this afternoon and defied all the whammies, all the jinxes, all the Yankees, even Mickey Mantle in a pinch-hitting role, and pitched a shutout to beat the Yankees for the first time since the Cardinals did it in nineteen hundred and forty-two.***

Corum also celebrates the amazing catch by Sandy Amoros in the 6th inning.

2:31:08 - ***"Little Sandy Amoros turned in one of the most wonderful plays you ever saw."***

Minutes later, Hall of Fame player Frankie Frisch is in the locker room with the Dodgers. Frisch is conducting interviews for the radio broadcast.

Walter O'Malley tells Frisch, ***"I'm delighted for all of our Brooklyn fans. At long last we've brought this world championship to Brooklyn."***

Pee Wee Reese tells Frisch, ***"How about that Podres Frank. Wasn't that tremendous?"***

The Morning Newspapers

The New York Daily News ran a giant banner headline on page 1 that read, ***"This is Next Year."***

In the New York Times on page 1 today, John Drebinger began his column 1 article with this, ***"Brooklyn's long cherished dream has finally come true. The Dodgers have won their first world series championship."***

That must have looked surreal to Brooklyn fans.

The Home News in New Brunswick, NJ, did a marvelous job capturing the moment. Jimmie Fleming started his article on the game with this, ***"The world***

stood still for one mad moment at 3:45 p.m. yesterday as Johnny Podres, Brooklyn southpaw wound up to throw the final pitch of the 1955 World Series. When that pitch to Yankee Elston Howard was tapped weakly to shortstop Pee Wee Reese, the ball game was over, the Brooks had won, 2 - 0, and the dream of a world championship, nurtured through 52 years, became a reality."

Across the country, Al Wolf of the Los Angeles Times had a watch that was 1 minute slower. He wrote, ***"At 3:44 p.m. today, every clock in Brooklyn stopped. Probably; some overwrought hearts did too. For at that instant, happy history was made and 30 years of frustration finally ended for all time. The Dodgers won their first World Series.***

Not even the completion of the Brooklyn Bridge which first linked that baseball-batty borough to the rest of these United States many long years ago, ranks as a comparable occasion.

This is THE day."

The MVP

Young Johnny Podres, one of the most unlikely candidates a week ago, was named the World Series MVP. And for good reason. Podres won game 3 in a complete game performance when the Dodgers were desperate for a win after losing games 1 and 2. And then he shut out the Yankees in game 7 in Yankee Stadium. It was a spirited performance from the 23-year-old.

In doing so, he became the first Dodgers' pitcher ever to win 2 games in a single World Series.

It's all the more remarkable when you consider that Podres had not completed a game in his last 13 starts in the regular season, and yet he completed both games he started in the World Series.

Yes, Johnny Podres was well deserving of the Most Valuable Player selection.

The Dodgers were struggling with pitchers as their two best starters, Don Newcombe and Carl Erskine, were limited to a combined 8 and 2/3 innings of work, in which they each had ERA's over 9.00!

Podres in his 2 starts, ended up pitching 18 of the 60 innings pitched by the entire staff (that's 36% of all the innings). Clem Labine was next on that list, pitching just half as many innings as Podres.

Johnny Podres was exuberant in the locker room after the game. The New York Times reported, ***"'Wow!' whooped Johnny, 'Wow, wow, wow! I'll never forget this all my life. What a wonderful thing - to win the world series.'"***

Then Podres yelled over to Pee Wee Reese, ***"Hey Pee Wee, what did I tell you? I said they wouldn't get a thing off me. Didn't I?"***

Podres had been confident before the game. He had, in fact, told Reese and reporters before game 7 that he would beat the Yankees.

And Podres told the Times that he wasn't nervous during the game, ***"No, I wasn't nervous. How could I be when the skipper told me he wanted me to pitch the seventh game and stood by me the way he did?"***

Podres was besieged by a bevy of reporters in the locker room, for Johnny was the man of the hour, the day, the week, the year, the decade, and the century for the Dodgers. He told the newspapermen, ***"My fast ball really had it. Mantle? I wasn't worried about him. I keep my fast ball up on him and he can't hit it... I was never worried about anybody."***

Then he yelled over to Pee Wee Reese, ***"Hey captain! What did I tell you? Go ahead tell them what I told you yesterday."*** And the captain complied, telling reporters, ***"You told me not to worry. You said you were going to shut them out."***

And shut out those damn Yankees he did.

Podres's father, Joseph, was so choked up by the victory that he had to leave the stadium right after the game so that he could sit ***"in his car outside for half an hour to compose himself,"*** according to Ross McGowen in the Times. He didn't want anyone to see him crying.

When Johnny Podres's father came into the locker room, Russ Meyer said to him, ***"Mr. Podres, you must be the proudest father in America. That kid of yours has more guts than the law allows."***

Tears of Joy

In addition to the senior Podres, some of the long time Dodgers were so overcome by the victory that they could not contain themselves either. McGowen reported, ***"Clem Labine... sat with bowed head. He looked up and smiled through the tears running down his cheeks. Imagine, a grown man crying."***

And Jim Ogle of the Newark Star-Ledger reported that Pee Wee Reese, ***"broke down and cried in the clubhouse."***

Dick Young in the New York Daily News reported that Johnny Podres wanted to cry but he couldn't. Young reported that Podres's uncle told him, ***"Go ahead John, cry, it's all right."***

Time for Reconciliation

McGowen also reported that Don Newcombe, who had gone on angry tirade during the season when Duke Snider filled his good hat with beer during a road trip in Milwaukee, now poured beer on his own head and posed with his arm around the Duke.

And Time for Reflection

Gil Hodges pointed to the Sandy Amoros catch and the ensuing double play as the key to the game. He told Jim Ogle, ***"That double play on Yogi Berra's fly to left broke their backs. Everything had to be perfect or we were in trouble - Sandy Amoros's catch, Pee Wee Reese's relay. Everything was."***

Typical of the soft-spoken, humble to the core Hodges, he didn't mention his all important contribution to that double play. It was Hodges who made the long stretch, while holding his foot on the 1st base bag, and adeptly made the low grab on Reese's throw just a millisecond before McDougald got there.

Dana Mozley in the Daily News agreed with Gil's assertion regarding the Amoros catch and throws as the most important moment. He wrote, ***"Certainly the one play that broke the Yankees' back was Sandy Amoros's great sixth-inning catch and resultant double play. He said an incoming wind held the ball just long enough for him to catch it."***

Amoros told Mozley, ***"I kept my eyes on the ball. I never looked at anything else."*** He was indicating he never looked at the stands that he would have crashed into if he had needed to go one more step.

The Scene in Brooklyn

The Newark Star-Ledger reported on what life was like in Brooklyn, 10 miles from Yankee Stadium, after the last out was made yesterday.

"Every auto horn in the borough began blasting, factory sirens started to shrill, and the voices of the delirious multitudes became screams... They locked up shop, boarded up the glass fronts and went on a baseball binge - all three million of them. Men and women danced in the streets."

Art Smith wrote an article in the Daily News that began, ***"Everything was crazy in Brooklyn last night... Nobody went home to supper. Nobody talked any sense... Everybody walked around with goofy expressions on their pans... For the unbelievable, the incredible, the impossible had come about. Them Dodgers had put them Yankees away under the Stadium sod and now they was champions of the whole world."***

Smith picked out examples of the pandemonium in his 2nd paragraph, ***"Candy store owners played the big treat to neighborhood kids who'd been robbing 'em for years... Women kissed neighbors they wouldn't be caught***

dead talking to... Never before had Brooklyn that borough of perennial October gloom gone so joyously screwy, so hysterically daffy, so ecstatically nuts."

Re-Visiting the Plays of the Game

Everyone who covered the game agreed that Sandy Amoros's catch on Yogi Berra's slicing fly ball to the left field corner was the play of the game and was the moment that "broke the Yankees' back."

Even Yankees' skipper Casey Stengel pointed to the Amoros catch as the Yankee killer. He told Jim McCulley in the Daily News, ***"the fella made a fine catch on the ball and if he hadn't of caught it, McDougald would have scored and we would have been tied."***

Instead, Berra was out on one of the great catches in World Series history and McDougald was doubled up after Amoros made a perfect throw to Reese who made a perfect throw to Hodges at 1st base. There were 2 outs, the Yankees were still 2 runs down, and Billy Martin was still stuck on 2nd base, when there could have been 2 runs in, a tie game, no outs and the go ahead run in scoring position.

The Sandy Amoros play quite possibly saved the World Series for the Dodgers.

I would also contend that Podres's strikeout of Bauer to end the 8th was of nearly equal significance. The Yankees had runners on 1st and 3rd. Bauer, represented the go ahead run. Podres threw the hardest pitch he had thrown in the entire game according to one sportswriter. Podres was under intense pressure and he came through, getting the man who had the highest batting average in the series, across both teams, to swing and miss.

And one more play that could have changed the complexion of the game if it had gone differently is worth re-visiting. In the bottom of the 3rd with the score still 0 – 0, the Yankees had Rizzuto on 2nd and Martin on 1st with 2 outs and Gil

McDougald the batter. McDougald ran the count full. A walk would load the bases for clean-up hitter, Yogi Berra, the best RBI man on the Yankees over the past 7 years.

On the payoff pitch, McDougald hit a sharp grounder to 3rd base that hit Rizzuto as he was nearing the bag. Rizzuto was out and the inning was over. But had the ball missed Rizzuto, he likely would have scored, putting the Yankees in the lead with Berra coming up and 2 men still on base.

That was an enormous break for the Brooklyn.

Podres's Poise

Indeed it was the poise that Podres exhibited in both games 3 and 7 that were the keys to Brooklyn's 1st ever World Series championship.

This morning, Podres penned an article in the Staten Island Advance and shared his inner most thoughts. He began, ***"I'm glad there's no law against happiness, because man, oh man, I'd sure be exceeding the legal limit."***

Then he shared the confidence he brought to Yankee Stadium yesterday, ***"I wasn't especially worried when Mickey Mantle came up as a pinch hitter with one on in the seventh inning. I simply kept the ball up on him and got him to pop the ball up to Pee Wee."***

That's remarkable. What 23-year-old wouldn't have been worried facing Mickey Mantle when one swing could tie the game, and the Mick had already homered off Podres back in game 3.

Podres also indicated his curve ball ***"wasn't especially good"*** in game 7. Podres wrote, ***"I let my fastball do most of the work."*** Again this is remarkable. Podres had been effective in game 3 because of his curve and his changeup. Without the curve, in the biggest game of his life, he adapted and over powered the Yankees in the house that Ruth built. It was just an astonishing performance by Podres.

Missing Mantle

Some writers pointed out that missing Mickey Mantle cost the Yankees the series. But this theory was debunked by Sid Ziff in today's Los Angeles Mirror. Yes, Mantle was unable to play in 4 of the 7 games. And yes, the Yankees had never played a World Series before in which either Ruth, DiMaggio, or Mantle had not started every game.

But the missing Mantle argument discounts the loss of Don Newcombe for the Dodgers. Pitchers are arguably more important than position players, and Newk played injured and was ineffective in game 1, and was not able to pitch for the rest of the series. If Newk had been in his midseason form, when he was a stunning 18 - 1, with a sub 3.00 ERA, he almost certainly would have won 2 games in the World Series. And consider this, Don Newcombe, an outstanding batter, actually had the highest batting average of every player on BOTH teams during the regular season.

Without Newcombe, as well as veteran pitcher Carl Erskine, who was also injured and only able to take the mound for just 3 innings, in which he yielded 3 runs, manager Walter Alston had to use 6 different starters in the first 6 games, a World Series record. And twice Alston had to send rookie starters to the mound. In fact, it's almost puzzling as to why Alston used all of the pitchers on his staff except for one, 19-year-old Sandy Koufax.

I contend that the Dodgers actually missed Newcombe more than the Yankees missed Mantle. It was the Dodgers who were at a personnel disadvantage in the series.

And so the Dodgers have finally won a World Series championship and it was well deserved.

Chapter Twenty-Six

The Daze After The World Series

I stuck around 1955 for another couple of weeks after the World Series before heading home to the present time. Some of the things I found out were fascinating.

The day after the newspapers reported the Dodgers had won their first World Series, Arthur Daley wrote a classic piece in his Sports of the Times column. He titled it, **"Flatbush Fantasy."** And he opened with this statement that brilliantly captured the dream-like moment for Dodgers fans, ***"There was an air of unreality to the recent world series. It was as if the script had been penned by Lewis Carroll after he'd acquired a feel for the job by writing Alice in Wonderland."***

While there was pandemonium in the borough of Brooklyn, as described at the end of the last chapter, there was no parade planned!

The players simply scattered after the World Series ended.

They didn't even get their World Series rings. In the ultimate irony, they would have to wait 'til next year, until opening day, to receive their hard earned World Series rings.

Fortunately, the players wouldn't have to settle for an organization ring, which had been the back-up plan by owner Walter O'Malley, in case the Dodgers had not won the series. In the foreword to this book is a great story about the organization rings as told by the 1955 Dodgers' TV and radio broadcast producer, Tom Villante.

Just knowing he would eventually receive an honest to goodness World Series ring was good enough for Carl Furillo. He told columnist Jimmy Cannon in Newsday on October 6th, ***"I could taste that ring. The years it took us."***

In the same article, Cannon also wrote, ***"This is the first time I've ever seen Gil Hodges excited."*** Hodges, the quietest Dodger, has been one of the bedrocks of the team since 1948, driving in over 100 runs in each of the past 7 seasons. Hodges told Cannon, ***We went out there and won it in the (Yankee) Stadium. That's what I like."***

The only players who stayed in Brooklyn after the World Series were Gil Hodges and Sandy Koufax. The October 5th Hartford Courant indicated these two were the only ones who made their year-round home in Brooklyn. And Koufax was the only Dodgers' player who had both been born in Brooklyn and graduated from high school in Brooklyn.

Although he didn't play in the 1955 World Series, this was actually the 2nd championship team Koufax had been on that was Brooklyn based. Three years earlier on October 9, 1952, the Brooklyn Daily Eagle newspaper reported that Koufax's sandlot team, the Tomahawks won the championship game in the Ice Cream League. Koufax was not the pitcher. He played 1st base. And he had the big hit in the title game. The Daily Eagle wrote one sentence about Koufax, ***"Sandy Koufax's triple with the bases loaded in the second inning was the payoff wallop."***

Here in 1955, not a single story focused on Koufax in the New York papers after the World Series until October 26th, when the New York Daily News announced that he had enrolled at Columbia University to take engineering classes.

While Koufax stuck around the city, Gil Hodges soon left Brooklyn for a trip to the Texas State Fair in the middle of October. On October 18th, an International News Service article reported Hodges was at the fair with Duke Snider and Carl Erskine. They were giving five daily baseball performances as well individual instruction in hitting and pitching. These types of appearance were a common way ball players, prior to the free agent era, could make much needed extra money in the offseason.

On October 23rd, a wire service photo showed the three Dodgers smiling and wearing big white cowboy hats at the fair.

Also with the three Dodgers' players at the Texas State Fair was Happy Felton serving as an emcee. During the season, Felton hosted the pre-game shows at Ebbets Field, called the Knothole Gang.

It was surprising to see Duke Snider at the Texas State Fair because the previous week, he completed a grueling cross-country drive from Brooklyn to his home in Lynwood, California, near Los Angeles. The Duke was pictured at his home in the Long Beach Independent on October 10th, as he got to meet his 3-week old son Kurt for the 1st time. Also pictured were his wife Beverly, 6-year-old son Kevin and 4-year-old daughter Pamela. He told the newspaper his immediate plans, ***"After a long auto trip from coast to coast, I think I'll just sleep for a week."***

Yet within a week, the Duke was back on the road to Texas. Such was life for major league ballplayers in the 1950s. Even one of the premier superstars of the game had to eke out a living.

The man of the hour, days and weeks after the World Series was of course the series MVP, Johnny Podres. An AP article on October 7th reported that Podres had arrived in his hometown of Witherbee in far upstate New York about 70 miles south of the Canadian border. It mentioned he drove into town in the new car that he had won for being World Series MVP, while his dad drove back home in the old family car.

The article also noted that Podres was resting up for a parade in Witherbee the next day. So there actually was a parade to celebrate the World Series victory somewhere.

Podres also had to do a little media damage control. Apparently, there had been a report that Johnny was engaged to an 18-year-old girl in the nearby town of Port Henry. But Johnny insisted that while he had gone on a few dates with the young lady, he presently had no girlfriend. For her part, the girl also confirmed that she was not engaged to Johnny Podres, and she had no idea how the rumor had gotten started.

The news for Jackie Robinson also involved damage control. Just two days after the World Series, on October 6th, Frank Eck of the Daily Sentinel in Rome, New York reported that Robinson was going to be facing a big pay cut for the 1956 season. Dodgers' GM Buzzie Bavasi told Eck, ***"He will get a contract deserving of a .256 hitter... I'm fed up with his popping off. He tells newspapermen he's coming in to see me about this and that. Well, why doesn't he come and see me before he pops off."***

Dodgers' manager Walter Alston was also upset with Jackie's penchant for protesting the manager's decisions in the press. Alston told Eck that Robinson, ***"had no business griping to the writers traveling with the team instead of first complaining to his manager."***

The Jackie Robinson situation is a complex one. By all objective standards, Robinson's output has declined. He did in fact bat .256, 40 points lower than any prior season in his career. And next year he'll be 37. But this is also a man who is the ultimate competitor on the field. His daring on the basepaths creates opportunities and unnerves his opponents. Even at his advanced age, he was the only player to steal home in the 1955 World Series.

In addition, his handling of pitchers while he is playing the infield is of immeasurable value. It was Jackie who kept putting positive thoughts in Podres's ear in the crucial game 3 when the Dodgers just had to win.

There has never been a player quite like Jackie Robinson. And it's a fact that the Dodgers' success in the last 9 seasons, started in 1947, when Robinson was a rookie. Only Reese has been a regular for longer. In Robinson's 9 seasons, the Dodgers have been a contender every year and won the pennant 5 times, after having won only a single pennant in the 26 seasons before Jackie joined the club.

NOTE from The Sports Time Traveler

I need to interrupt this chapter for one minute to write to you from the present time. Recently I read Carl Erskine's book, "What I Learned from Jackie Robinson." It's a short and sensational read.

In the book, Erskine recounts how after 9 years of close calls, Jackie Robinson savored the 1955 World Series victory. Carl wrote, *"Jackie, I know, felt that this one was special. And he knew that one day there would be volumes written about this 1955 World Series, and our storied team."*

In addition to being one of the great players in baseball history, Jackie Robinson, of course, will always be remembered as the man who broke color barrier in baseball. But Carl Erskine felt that his teammate Jackie deserved more accolades than just what he's received for his impact in the sports world. Carl wrote this about Jackie, *"I believe Jackie single-handedly kicked off the civil rights movement, but it would have been nice if someone phrased it that way."*

Carl, wherever you are, I've just taken your call to action.

Now back to 1955.

Robinson was embroiled in another controversy a few days later, that was not of his making in any way. Frank Kellert, the Dodgers' reserve 1st baseman, ignited the brouhaha after he was sold to the Chicago Cubs a few days after the conclusion of the World Series.

A week earlier, Kellert had been pinch-hitting in the top of the 8th inning in game 1 of the series, when Jackie Robinson stole home. Kellert had the closest view of the play besides the umpire.

Jackie Robinson's steal of home was one of the most daring and exciting plays of the entire World Series.

NOTE from The Sports Time Traveler

I need to interrupt this chapter once again to inform you that Jackie Robinson remains the last player to ever steal home in a World Series game in which he was the only runner on base, and thus was not simply part of a double steal play.

And no one else stole home in World Series play, that was not part of a double steal, going all the way back to 1921.

In the last 105 years, only Jackie Robinson has had a solo steal of home in a World Series game.

Now let's return again to 1955.

A week after the World Series, Kellert, now suddenly a member of the Chicago Cubs, decided to reveal to the Associated Press that Jackie was really out on the play - in his opinion.

Kellert went on to tell the AP that he was thanked by Jackie Robinson for his help on the play. Robinson, he said, had thanked him for ***"helping cloak the play by standing in tight at the plate and making Berra reach across for the tag."***

Yankees' catcher Yogi Berra, who had applied the tag, naturally would have agreed with Kellert. While Robinson himself had told reporters he was safe, ***"No doubt about it in my mind at all."***

But the fact is that ruling rested with umpire Bill Summers who had called Robinson safe.

And several days later, on October 20th, Dick Young writing in the New York Daily News tackled this controversy in depth with a stinging rebuke of Kellert. Young began his article with this assessment of Kellert's claim that Jackie was out at the plate, ***"IT SOUNDED LIKE A WELL SQUEEZED BUNCH of sour grapes."***

Young had seen the play live and studied photographs and was certain that Jackie was safe at home. He also discounted Kellert's recollection of the play, ***"Persons involved in swift happenings often are the poorest judges of***

what truly occurred. They become more excited than does the uninvolved observer. Therefore, as close as Kellert was to the play, in his roles as batter, his conception of the play does not necessarily have to be any better than mine."

Dick Young concluded his article writing, ***"Kellert is entitled to his popoff, though. He did a fine one year job on the bench for the Brooks."***

NOTE from The Sports Time Traveler

Yet again, I have to interrupt this chapter to inform you that I am in agreement that Kellert's kvetching about the call at the plate has no credence. If you watch the play on YouTube you will see that Kellert does not *"cloak the play"* as he said in 1955, in fact he stepped away on the play, making it easier for Berra and more difficult for Jackie. This lack of memory of his own actions invalidates his recollection of the tag on Robinson at home.

In addition, the play at the plate was extremely close. This viewer agrees with Dick Young and the umpire, that Jackie Robinson was safe. But regardless of what I think, our criteria here in the present time is that the call on the field stands unless there is definitive evidence to overturn it, and in this case there clearly is no grounds in the video or pictures to overturn the call.

Now again, we return to 1955.

There was yet another controversy being extinguished right after the World Series. This one involving the owner Walter O'Malley. Just a day after the newspapers described the delirium in Dodger land, the Newark Star-Ledger's John Craig declared, ***" Podres' 2-0 victory places Brooklyn atop the baseball world today and should end all rumors that the franchise will be shifted elsewhere."***

Craig expressed relief as he wrote, ***"Perhaps the Dodgers will move to a new ball park in the future, possibly a park closer to the potential drawing power in Queens, Nassau and Suffolk, but move off Long Island? Never!"***

Craig provided some context for the story indicating that, ***"O'Malley has made it clear for months that he has no intention of moving the Dodgers out of Brooklyn but he needs the cooperation of city officials to condemn land for a new ball park."***

Craig concluded that winning game 7 saved the Dodgers from moving out of Brooklyn.

A day later even happier news was reported in the Newark Star-Ledger. An AP article indicated that telephone calls to the Brooklyn Dodgers' offices which previously were greeted with, ***"Brooklyn Dodgers,"*** were now being answered with, ***"World Champions,"*** by the switchboard operator.

On the same day, October 7th, The New York Daily News reported how the Dodgers had agreed to divvy up the World Series shares. Players on the World Series roster would receive $9,768 each. For the younger players, including 25-year-old Sandy Amoros, that was more money than they made in the entire season.

Several players, who had spent some time with the club earlier in the season, were voted lesser shares. Tom Lasorda received one of those lesser shares. Lasorda was a lefty pitcher who had started the season with the Dodgers, and appeared in just 4 games for a grand total of just 4 innings, during which he gave up 6 earned runs. He was sent down to Montreal in June. Lasorda was also the player who came back from his home to pitch batting practice before game 1 of the World Series. Tom Lasorda received $1,000.

By the way, when Lasorda was sent to Montreal it was to make the required room for the bonus baby, Sandy Koufax. Koufax, of course, received a full share. Even though he didn't play in the World Series, Koufax was on the World Series roster, and he was the only pitcher on the roster to not see any World Series activity.

Also on October 7th, but 700 miles west in Kentucky, Pee Wee Reese, the captain of the Dodgers and affectionately known as "The Little Colonel," was back in his home state, where the newspapers reported that this day was designated as Pee Wee Reese Day. The proclamation had been made the day prior by Kentucky governor Lawrence Wetherby. The governor had commended Reese for exhibiting, ***"the highest standards of sportsmanship."*** Sportswriter Bill Thompson, of the Lexington Herald wrote, ***"A special day for a more worthy person couldn't be proclaimed. It is my opinion (and you can take it for what it's worth) that Reese had just as much to do with Brooklyn's march to the National League championship and over the New York Yankees in the World Series as any man on the squad - in fact, perhaps a little more."***

A day later there was already speculation on the 1956 World Series. A United Press article forecasted the Yankees and the Dodgers would clash again in the Fall Classic in '56.

The Dodgers, by the Fall of '56, would have many key players over 30 years old including:

37 – Pee Wee Reese

37 – Jackie Robinson

34 – Roy Campanella

34 – Carl Furillo

32 – Gil Hodges

But the Dodgers' starting pitchers in all 7 games in 1955 were under 30 years old, and two of their top relievers Clem Labine and Don Bessent were also under 30. The Dodgers were seen as loaded with pitching going into next year.

The thinking was that the pitching would carry the Dodgers back to the World Series in 1956.

One of those young pitchers of course would be the freshly named World Series MVP Johnny Podres, who had just turned 23 during the series. And Podres was enjoying his momentary fame. On October 13th, newspapers around the country carried a picture of Podres wearing a dress!

The AP wire photo showed Podres rearing back to throw a fastball with his left hand, and his right leg high in the air, revealing his petticoat skirt underneath his gown. What was going on?

Johnny Podres was a guest on the popular television show on ABC called "Masquerade Party." The show featured famous people wearing disguises and a celebrity panel that had to ask questions to figure out who the person was. In this case, the producers outfitted Podres to look like Revolutionary War figure Molly Pitcher, a very appropriate choice given Podres's profession. I didn't get to watch the show, so if anyone recalls whether Podres was able to fool the panel the way he fooled Yankees' hitters please let me know.

That concludes my journey to experience the 1955 Brooklyn Dodgers. I hope you enjoyed traveling back in time with me.

Please email me at Len@fermaninnovation.com to share your feedback.

ADDITIONAL BOOKS BY THE SPORTS TIME TRAVELER

You can find all my books on Amazon, including these two:

The 1973 Mets – You've Got to Believe

Experience the magic of the 1973 Mets iconic "Ya Gotta Believe" season. The 1973 Mets provided some of the most dramatic heart-warming moments in sports history with their dash from last place to the World Series in a miraculous six week stretch. The reader will have the opportunity to share in the excitement of this incredible baseball season which was also the final year in the career of the legendary Willie Mays.

The book has been accepted into the National Baseball Hall of Fame museum and library collection in Cooperstown, NY.

Great Golf Tournaments – Volume 1

Follow 27 great golf tournaments that were each played more than 50 years ago and featured many of the top golfers in the game's history. Some of these tournaments were so gripping that they're routinely recalled by television broadcasters and sportswriters today, such as the 1975 Masters. Others have been seemingly forgotten, yet offer no less sensational drama, like the 1964 Western Open. All of them are told in a style designed to make you feel the emotions of the golfers and fans, as though you're there following the action. The suspense builds until you find out who wins at the nail-biting conclusion of each chapter.

The book received a fantastic review in Forbes magazine in December, 2025. You can find the review by typing in "Great Golf Tournaments Forbes" in a Google search.

Please email me at Len@fermaninnovation.com to share your feedback.

www.ingramcontent.com/pod-product-compliance
Lightning Source LLC
LaVergne TN
LVHW090603110826
845146LV00001B/242
9798991501248